John Knox House

Gateway to Edinburgh's Old Town

DONALD SMITH

JOHN DONALD PUBLISHERS LTD
EDINBURGH

ISBN 0 85976 437 0

The publisher acknowledges subsidy from
the Scottish Arts Council towards the
publication of this volume.

British Library Cataloguing in Publication Data

A catalogue record for this book is available
from the British Library.

Typeset by WestKey Ltd., Falmouth
Printed and bound in Great Britain by Bell & Bain Ltd., Glasgow

PREFACE AND ACKNOWLEDGEMENTS

This book was not born out of dilettante curiosity or a passion for historical knowledge, but out of practical necessity. The need was to base the renaissance of the Netherbow site in today's Old Town on as good an understanding of the physical and cultural history of the area as we could possibly obtain.

This was inevitably a collaborative venture because the Old Town brings people together to achieve the best. Sir Jamie Stormonth-Darling, Brigadier James Wilson and Jim Johnson of the then Edinburgh Old Town Committee for Conservation and Renewal, and its related Edinburgh Old Town Charitable Trust, were key supporters. The Netherbow's own Chairman David Maxwell was a constant encouragement in the early stages and throughout, while the Reverend Dr Ian Doyle of The Church of Scotland's Board of National Mission saw the logic from the beginning, and held steady through the ups and downs of Church committees.

Another set of people provided the expertise, not least Benjamin Tindall and Iain Stewart of Benjamin Tindall Architects. But others including Ian Low, Jim Lennie, Zoë Hall, Jim Gilhooley, Anne Maxwell, Ian Fraser, Mark Collard the City Archaeologist, Harry Linley the retired Curator, and Dr Charles Kelham all provided vital pieces of the jigsaw. The National Museums of Scotland, The National Library of Scotland, The National Monument Record, the Edinburgh City Archives and the Central Library provided their help generously and professionally, as did the contractors and George Young, Campbell and Smith's splendid site foreman. I also benefited from Kenneth Freeman Mosman's commitment to his family's history.

But without the hard work of The Netherbow's own staff the whole enterprise could not have been sustained and no-one from that generous team, past and present, will grudge me mentioning in particular The Netherbow's distinguished succession of secretaries, Frances Handford and Kay Shanks.

The venture though was worthwhile because the people of Edinburgh are seriously interested in the history of their town and take a pride in sharing it with visitors, because they believe that in telling the city's story they are telling you something real about themselves.

Edinburgh, 1996   D.S.

A VOICE FROM KNOX'S CORNER NETHERBOW

Ye douce auld-farrant Edinbro' folks
Fling by your taunts, your jeers, and jokes
Love ye the roof-tree o' John Knox?
Then act thegither
An' dinna flee like fechtin' cocks
At ane anither.

A' ye wha's love wad still defend me!
A' ye wha helpin' han's wad lend me,
'Ere wintry storms or ruins rend me,
O! grant my prayer.
An' sen' a hundred men to mend me
An' fecht nae mair.

— *The Scotsman*, 6 August 1849

CONTENTS

To my parents

CHAPTER ONE

THE HOUSE IN THE NETHERBOW

Looking east down Edinburgh's Royal Mile, the building now known as John Knox House juts out, disrupting the broad street and imposing its presence between the viewer and the distant shoreline of Aberlady Bay. In the 1850s and again in the 1950s it was suggested that the house be demolished to allow freer access to the bustling High Street, first for horse-drawn traffic and then for the omnipresent car. Fortunately John Knox House clung stubbornly to its original site, a witness to the fundamental geography of this remarkable city as well as a very significant part of its history.

The Royal Burgh of Edinburgh extended from the Castle rock down the spine or ridge of the Castle hill as far as its main gate, the Netherbow Port. To the north the town was bounded by a steep incline and the Nor Loch; to the south the buildings descended to the Cowgate and then spilled out towards Arthur's Seat. Beyond the Netherbow, continuing in a straight line eastwards, you reached the independent burgh of the Canongate which developed in association with the Abbey of Holyrood.

Turning left outside the Netherbow you joined Leith Wynd, the road to Edinburgh's port on the Firth of Forth and beyond that the sea, clearly visible from the gateway itself.

The length of the burgh from Castle to Netherbow was established early. There is a reference to the 'arcus inferior' or nether bow in a charter of 1369, but the basic structure of the town probably dates to the 12th century. The raison d'etre of the Scottish medieval burgh was its right to hold markets and it was this function which dictated the layout of the streets with the provision of at least one open market space. The Church also had a central position as the focus of social, cultural and religious life, while, in Edinburgh's case, a third determining factor was the need for a strong defensive position against English incursions.

The early Scottish burgh however retained a rural as well as urban character, linking it directly to the agricultural communities which it served. Each house had its own landholding for pigs, goats, poultry and crops such as beans, kail and bere or barley. Common grazings existed around the burgh and in the 12th and 13th centuries only the walls would distinguish Edinburgh from a substantial village. Contemporary historians reckon that in the 13th century the main Scottish burghs consisted of 3–400 houses and a population not exceeding 1,000 people.

These early town-villages were built in timber except for their public buildings and it was not until the mid-15th century that houses began to be built in stone. By this period, despite the intervening ravages of the Black Death, Scotland was experiencing what could fairly be described as urban growth. For Edinburgh this involved an increase in trade, particularly overseas trade, a very favourable 'special relationship' with the monarchy, and the expansion of the Scottish Church in specifically urban forms such as friaries, hospices and endowed chapels attached to the burgh church. It is at this point of 15th century urban growth that we can make the first tentative links between the development of Edinburgh and the physical structure of the surviving house in the Netherbow.

The building now described as John Knox House consists of not one but two late-medieval Scottish 'lands' or town houses. The building seen jutting out into the High Street is the 'foreland' and contains on two upper floors a single generously proportioned room or 'hall' with adjacent small 'chambers' which are built on timber jetties or galleries projecting out over the street from the main walls. Above these two floors is a more modest 'loft house' or upper flat, while below is a suite of small shops or booths on street level, and below that again an extensive cellar. Concealed by this rather grand foreland is a much more traditional and older Scottish house which became, with the construction of its finer neighbour, a humble 'backland'.

Originally the backland had two storeys with a hall and chamber (front and back room) on each level. However because of the way in which the ground falls away on the north side the ground floor of the backland is approximately equivalent to the cellars of the foreland. In addition, to complicate the picture, the back room on the second floor has been lost (probably demolished as ruinous in the late 19th century), while a further two rooms have been added on top of the original front room!

This chequered history, which we will explore further in due course, has led to the confused view that the backland was a later addition rather than the older building. But the rubble walls exposed in the investigation of 1990–91, and the blocked-in windows suggest construction before any house existed on the foreland site. This sequence also makes sense of the way in which the spiral or 'turnpike' stair on the west side struggles to provide separate access to the two houses on each floor and accommodate the different levels of foreland and backland. Despite later attempts to rationalize each floor throughout the building by adjusting the backland levels, observant visitors to the house today will notice that there is an increasing disparity between the levels of the front and back rooms the further they go up the building.

Equally interesting is the way in which the backland aligns with the original frontage of Moubray House next door which also dates to the 15th century. In combination the backland of the Netherbow house and Moubray's land clearly delineate the building line of the medieval market street. In comparison with the foreland and Moubray's the backland is a poor relation. It has no exceptional artistic or architectural features but it should be commended by both its typicality and its age. Other houses of the same kind were routinely dispensed with but the backland of the Netherbow may be among the first stone-built domestic buildings in Edinburgh.

Precise dating of such buildings is notoriously difficult but in the case of the backland we have a vital clue: the present building, or at least its original core, was constructed before any house existed on the foreland site. Can the foreland provide us with a firmer date?

There is clear evidence of at least two major phases of construction on the foreland site. The later of these is associated with the Mossmans, a prominent family of goldsmiths. A remarkable amount of information (not least the house itself!) survives to illuminate both the causes and the results of that construction in the late 1550s which we shall consider in Chapter Three. But the Mossmans did not build on an empty site; they substantially reconstructed an earlier house which came into their possession through the marriage of James Mossman to the heiress Mariota Arres in 1556.[1] Even a cursory examination of the internal walls of the foreland uncovered in 1991 reveals a large blocked-up fireplace one side of which has been covered over by a new gable wall. Archaeological evidence confirms the foreland cellars as of earlier construction than the 1556 house. So when was the first house erected on the prominent and unusual foreland site?

This breaking of the rules, building out beyond the street line and encroaching on the public market space, must be connected with the Netherbow Port and the fortifications of the medieval town. This however still leaves a wide field of dates since major alterations to the town walls and/or the Netherbow Port were carried out in or soon after 1472, 1513, 1558 and 1571, not to mention the largely ignored royal decree of 1450 about Edinburgh's walls and the likelihood that urgent remedial work was required after the successful English attack on the town in 1544.

In fact all of the 16th century dates listed above are associated with some crisis in the affairs of the burgh and reflect hurried action in response to imminent danger, as in the aftermath of the defeat at Flodden in 1513 or in the run-up to the assault by the Protestant Lords of the Congregation in 1559. These were hardly times at which repairs or alterations to the city's defences could be linked with a new housing development. In addition the later dates come after the Mossmans' rebuilding of the house on the foreland site. Repairs after 1544 are much more likely but do not account for the first construction on the foreland since, as we shall see, there is documentary evidence linking Mariota Arres, the bride-to-be of 1556, with the site well before 1544.

A royal charter of 1450 enjoins the citizens of Edinburgh to 'fosse, bulwark, wall, toure, turate, and otherwise to strengthen our burgh against the dreid, the evil and the skaith of our auld enemyis of England'. This is not to suppose that these were Edinburgh's first walls since there are earlier references to the King's Walls. Nor is it to presume that the job was carried through since in 1472 a much stronger edict is issued instructing the same work on pain of forfeiture and loss of burgh citizenship for anyone reluctant to pay their share.

The 1472 charter produced action. The wall was repaired and/or rebuilt along a line approximately midway between the High Street and the Cowgate. The reconstruction of the Netherbow Port however seems to have posed some problems. This was probably because the burgh had spilled out beyond the original gate and also because the broad market street offered no natural closure which could reinforce and protect this principal means of access into the city.

A prominent burgess, Alexander Boncle, stepped in to create a strong gatehouse set in a narrow passage by building a row of four houses with very thick walls. In this way he turned the Netherbow into a short narrow street ending on the west or upper side with the Netherbow Port. This action reveals Boncle as a patriot but also as a businessman since each house was to be provided with booths or shops on the ground floor and the most prominent house at the top end was assigned to Boncle's own son-in-law Walter Reidpath, a goldsmith. The Netherbow was a critical defensive feature but the new street was also a prime commercial site through which most of those leaving and entering the burgh had to pass.

The bones of this account were first set out by Dr Charles Malcolm, an historian and Signet librarian whose unpublished Rhind Lectures on 'The Buildings of Edinburgh' (1937) seem to have gone astray in the relevant Edinburgh libraries, but whose later account of the history of John Knox House survives in typescript.[2] Malcolm's account was vindicated in 1993 when during alterations to the pavement in front of The Netherbow Arts Centre the street line of Boncle's Netherbow was revealed beneath the paving slabs.

The effects of Boncle's investment can be seen in every 18th and 19th century map of Edinburgh where the Netherbow is clearly a separate narrow section of the High Street stretching from the present John Knox House to the corner of Leith Wynd. The only difference in the pattern is that the Netherbow Port was transferred after 1513 from the top to the bottom end of the Netherbow and then in 1764 demolished. Although today Leith Wynd has also gone the survival of the house in the Netherbow or John Knox House maintains to some extent the configuration of 1472 as well as the much earlier location of the 'arcus inferior'.[3]

Walter Reidpath died sometime after 1511 and sometime before 1525 the house in the Netherbow became the property of Walter's daughter Christina.[4] Christina in her turn passed the house on in 1525 to her son John Arres, and it was John's daughter Mariota who was to marry James Mossman in 1556 taking the house as part of her marriage portion. Hence an unbroken line of possession links the Boncle construction of post-1472 with the property which the Mossmans set about rebuilding after 1556, whatever additional repairs may have intervened between these dates. It has not often been noticed that this succession gives a chronological framework for the buildings on the present John Knox House site, as well as a reference point for the dating and location of Edinburgh's most important gatehouse. It is also worth remarking that the next door house (second in line eastwards on the Netherbow) also came into the ownership of the Reidpaths, illustrating the way in which family property holdings were assiduously consolidated and extended.

But can this documentary record, scrupulously maintained in the daybooks of Edinburgh's notaries, be related directly to the existing buildings of the house in the Netherbow? The backland is a pre-1472 market street stonebuilt house, originally two storeys tall, which survives in a reduced form to the present. Joining the backland to the Mossman construction of post-1556 is a massive gable wall 1m 33cm thick at ground level. This gable rises to three storeys and on the third storey two huge corbels (now enclosed by a later backland addition) adorn the rear wall.

This surviving wall bears the hallmarks of the semi-fortified construction of 1472 beside the newly strengthened Netherbow Port. It is in this wall that the partially built over fireplace is set on the ground floor, and it is this gable which lends strength to both foreland and backland. After all why demolish such a thorough and expensive piece of building when it is structurally supporting one house and can be readapted to support a new adjoining house? The gable provides a mark of physical continuity just as the notaries preserved the legal connection from generation to generation.

If this scenario is correct then it is also likely that the backland and foreland formed one property holding from the time of the 1472 development. This is because the addition of the foreland would have devalued the backland as an independent asset blocking its light and cramping its street access. Unified ownership would not prevent the property being used as two and probably more dwelling houses as need and family convenience dictated. The documentary record suggests one holding from the start and there is no later reference to the addition of the backland or, as far as I can ascertain, to the backland as an independent property.

The physical and documentary integrity of this site and its buildings provide a unique viewpoint or window on the social, cultural and economic life of the period. It is also our best focus for a remarkable family story leading through the Arres heiress to the rise and fall of the Mossman goldsmiths.

NOTES

1. *Protocol Book of Alexander King*, 27 July 1556.
2. See *John Knox House*, an unfinished typescript by Dr Charles Malcolm with manuscript notes, deposited in the Edinburgh Room of the City's Central Library.
3. *Protocol Book of Vincent Strachan*, 22 December 1525. The period from 1470 was one of rapid urban growth. For the development of the early Scottish burghs see M. Lynch, M. Spearman and G. Stell (eds.) *The Scottish Medieval Town* (Edinburgh, 1988).

CHAPTER TWO

THE HEIRESS

In the medieval burgh of Edinburgh, the houses were called lands, while the combined holding of a land with its accompanying strip of ground was known as a tenement. The possession of this holding conferred the right of citizenship or 'burgess-ship' on the owner. In royal burghs such as Edinburgh the initial grants of holdings were made directly by the King, but both the rights of property and so of citizenship soon became a matter of inheritance.

Ownership of a house in the burgh was not just about security and shelter, or even of the combined living and working space which most houses provided. Each holding also conferred social position, access to the trading privileges and monopolies of the burgh, and the right to a voice in the 'community of the burgh'. As towns grew this last right was exercised as a vote in election of a Council. Small surprise therefore that ownership and the passing on of property became the prevailing concern of burgh society as the volume of even the surviving legal records confirms. Small wonder also that the fastest growing and most upwardly mobile professional group in burgh society were the lawyers.

How did Mariota Arres come to own the house in the Netherbow, and how were her rights affected by her marriage to the goldsmith James Mossman in 1556.

In the first chapter we traced the ownership of this prime property to the intervention of Alexander Boncle in the reconstruction of Edinburgh's walls and gatehouse after 1472. The Boncles were a wealthy merchant family, and the Merchant Guilds represented the economic elite of burgh society which also, despite pressure from the Craft Guilds, retained political control of the Town Councils. The wealthier merchants were also landowners, buying and often marrying into the gentry or laird class and into the nobility. A remarkable image of Boncle wealth and influence is preserved in the Trinity Altarpice (now on permanent display in the National Gallery of Scotland) in which Alexander's uncle, Sir Edward Boncle, appears kneeling in the foreground – the pious patron of the Queen Dowager's collegiate church of 1462. It is typical of both Scottish trade connections and aspirations that the altarpiece was commissioned from one of Europe's greatest artists, the Fleming, Hugo van der Goes.

The house in the Netherbow was assigned by Boncle to his son-in-law Walter Reidpath the goldsmith. The goldsmiths were Craftsmen rather than Merchants, but occupied an unusual position by virtue of the exclusivity and the opulence of their trade. Goldsmiths were often pawnbrokers and moneylenders as well, and the professional expertise and business connections of the Edinburgh goldsmiths were central to the operation of the Royal Mint and the maintenance of the national coinage. To some extent they performed the functions of later banking institutions. In the 1470s the goldsmiths formed a small elite within the Guild of Hammermen, later forming a fully independent Craft Guild in 1525.

Walter Reidpath's acquisition of this house, consequent upon his prudent marriage into the Boncle family, assured his position as a prosperous Edinburgh burgess, and gave him a strategically sited place of business. The ground floor provided him with two or three booths or shops. One of these would be retained to front the goldsmith business though most important transactions would be conducted in private in the house above or at the client's home. The other shops would be let out to be used by other Craftsmen. There would be no difficulty in letting on a site so conveniently situated beside the main city gate, and such booths, albeit small in size, were a highly valued commercial asset.

The economic importance placed upon the house in the Netherbow is reflected in the way the property was kept in the Reidpath family, through both male and female ownership. In 1525 Walter's daughter Christina passed the house on to her son John Arres. She had probably received the house as part of her marriage settlement and her granddaughter Mariota, who inherited the house through her father's death, also maintained a life interest in the property through her own marriage settlement. John Arres, Christina's husband, was a Barber Surgeon by craft and may have practised his trade from the house, but it was as a Reidpath, with the consent of her husband, that Christina transferred ownership of the family home to their son and joint heir, the second John Arres.

Carefully recorded by the family notary, the transaction of 1525 was a typical family settlement in anticipation of the grim reaper[1]. Although ownership was transferred to the next generation the liferent was retained by Christina and her husband, or whoever lived longer. So while the parents were comfortably provided with a house or, if necessary, income from its let, John Arres junior secured the privileges of burgess status and the opportunity to develop his own future prosperity. By 1525 Christina must have been in her fifties – a respectable old age in the early 16th century – and the likelihood is that she lived on in the house in which she had been brought up for only a few years longer.

Of the second John Arres we know very little, except that on 10 January 1555 the house in the Netherbow became the property of his daughter and Christina's granddaughter, Mariota, due to his death[2]. On the same day as her formal inheritance, and with the approval of her guardians, Mariota leased the house to the goldsmith John Mossman and his second wife Isobel Dee. There is no record of an Arres son though Mariota did have a sister Barbara, who married the goldsmith James Cockie. Given the later history of the house the continuing strength of the goldsmith connection is significant.

It is interesting to speculate what changes Walter Reidpath's house had undergone in the intervening period. These were years of economic growth in Edinburgh and improvements can be presumed, as well as vicissitudes such as the English attack in 1544, which in their turn became the spur for further improvements. The surviving physical record suggests changes, as we have already seen, but until 1555 the documentary record also implies, without guaranteeing, continuity. The house was an important property which the family tended to live in and trade from rather than let. Of course, with the death of John Arres junior leaving two unmarried daughters, there was no immediate prospect of continuity and the vacuum had to be filled by alliance with another family. However to understand the negotiations and transactions which ensued we need to know more about the background to Mariota's legal and financial position following her father's death.

The medieval Scottish burgh was in many respects a patriarchal society and the role of women was primarily domestic. However, since the household economy coincided to a large extent with the workplace economy (as we have already seen in the case of the

John Knox House and the Netherbow Street frontage from the print by Thomas H. Shepherd, 1829.

John Knox House and Balmerino's House from a drawing by T. Allom, published in *Caledonia Illustrated* (1838).

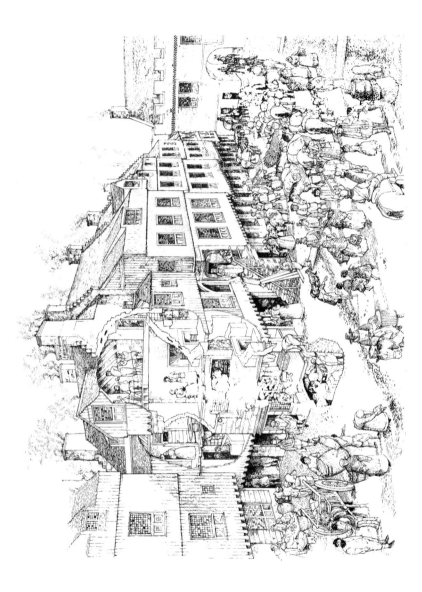

John Knox House and the Netherbow in 1600. Reconstruction drawing by David Simon (1990).

The Netherbow Port from the East, drawn from older prints by Daniel Wilson and engraved by W. Forrest. Published in Wilson's *Memorials of Edinburgh in the Olden Time* (1886). The Port was dismantled in 1764.

The Netherbow Port from the West, from an original drawing in the Queen's Prints and drawings in the British Museum published in *Old and New Edinburgh* by James Grant (no date).

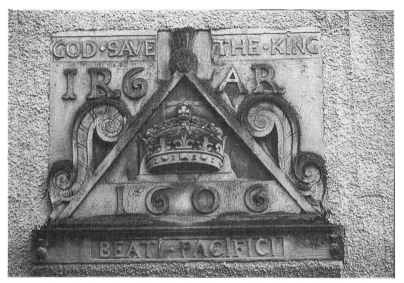

The sculptured plaque from The Netherbow Port, now located in the Netherbow Arts Centre courtyard. Dated 1606, the plaque bears the initials of James VI and Queen Anne, and commemorates a planned royal visit to Edinburgh which did not in fact take place. Photograph by Anne Maxwell.

The Oak Room on the second floor of John Knox House which contains early panelling, the painted ceiling, and a section of a painted ceiling from the Dean Mansion, now wall mounted. Photograph by Simon Jones.

Details drawn from the early 16th-century painted ceiling. The rumbustious mixture of motifs is probably the result of local craftsmen and clients selecting from pattern books. They in their turn reflect a northern European fashion of the grotesque. Drawing by Iain Stewart.

French print illustrating a 16th-century mint. The use of dies and punches made the mint mobile to the extent that James Mosman was able to produce a Marian coinage in Edinburgh Castle during the siege.

A plan of the siege of Edinburgh Castle, May 1573, published in Holinshed's *Chronicle*.

The only portrait of John Knox which is likely to be authentic. Published in *Icones* in Geneva in 1580, the portrait by Theodore Beza is probably based on a 'likeness' which he requested from Scotland.

house in the Netherbow), this was not a tightly circumscribed sphere of interest. Moreover the economic role of women of the burgess class was underpinned by their legal rights. Elizabeth Euan, a recent historian of the medieval Scottish burgh, puts it succinctly:

> Inheritance was not restricted to the eldest son. If a burgess' only child was a daughter she had the same rights of inheritance as an eldest child. She could also pass on the rights of burgess-ship and membership of the guild to her husband.[3]

The rights of the widow and children of a burgess were also protected. The burgh laws assigned the widow the inner half of the family house for the rest of her life. In addition many women enjoyed 'grants for life' of property and money made by their husbands in their wills. Equally and most importantly, any property and money brought into the joint ownership of husband and wife as part of a marriage settlement reverted automatically to the woman after her husband's death. Even during her husband's lifetime the woman retained a clear joint interest in these assets which could not be alienated by sale or transfer without her agreement. Hence the willingness of families to provide for their daughters on marriage property and money which not only promoted a beneficial match but gave lifelong economic security. In the absence of life assurance, property offered the best longterm personal investment.

The main purpose of these rules was to preserve burgess-ships intact and to prevent the dissipation of property with the subsequent weakening of social status and the economic fabric of the burgh. Religious and humanitarian motives however also played a part and it is noteworthy that one of the main activities of the Guilds, which were religious as well as economic organisations, was the care of the dependents of deceased members of the Craft. Whatever the motives the strategy tended to work, since many burgess families acquired additional properties, consolidating their position and greatly increasing family wealth in the 16th century burgh. The benefits to women were to some extent a by-product but they do explain the circumstances in which a wealthy widow, Janet Rynd, was able to contribute £2,000 to complete the Magdalen Chapel in the Cowgate in the early 1540s.

They also explain why, on her father's death, Mariota Arres, though still a minor in need of guardians, was a woman of property, possessing two houses in Liberton Wynd, two in Forrester's Wynd, one in the High Street, and one in the Netherbow – excluding money and movable goods. The interests of the heiress required protection; and a priest, George Littlejohn, and a goldsmith, Alexander Mossman, were appointed to act as guardians. Their principal job would be to arrange a satisfactory marriage, by which burgh society meant a socially advantageous and financially prudent alliance.

The recurrence of the name Mossman in the documents of 1555, once as a guardian in the shape of Alexander, and once as lessee of the Netherbow house, in the shape of John, suggests that a satisfactory candidate on both counts would not be far to seek.

NOTES

1. *Protocol Book of Vincent Strachan*, 22 December 1525.
2. *Protocol Book of Alexander King*, 10 January 1555.
3. E. Euan *Town Life in Fourteenth-Century Scotland* (Edinburgh, 1990) p. 93.

CHAPTER THREE

THE GOLDSMITH'S MARRIAGE

The goldsmiths of Edinburgh formed an elite group within the Guild of the Hammermen or metalworkers. In 1525 they founded their own independent Guild, though it is likely that they had already been operating together within the older entity[1]. Even in 1558 there were 14 goldsmiths in Edinburgh and by 1583 the number had only risen to 19. By reason of wealth and exclusivity they were a tight-knit, influential caste whose corporate structures have survived to this day when the Guild system in general is moribund.

The first minute-book of the Edinburgh goldsmiths, begun in 1525, also survives along with the register of members. Among the first forty names are five Mossmans. The first, Alan Mossman, is number four while James, Mariota's prospective husband, is number 40. James' father, John Mossman, is number 19 and Mariota's guardian, Alexander, is number 23. After James comes James Cockie (number 47) who married Mariota's sister, three more John Mossmans, and finally at number 67 another James Mossman. Among this latter group are James' brother and his nephew – both John Mossmans – who were to become the mainstay of the family's goldsmithing traditions. Even for a clannish burghal society the Mossmans constituted a notable family grouping. It is also apparent why Mariota Arres' wealth and goldsmith connections put her in the relatively restricted target area of 'desirable match'.

Of the Mossman goldsmiths James and his father John were the most distinguished representatives. This eminence can be dated at least to 1539 when during the reign of James V John Mossman was appointed 'wardane of our soverane lordis cunze for all the dais of his lyfe'[2]. This lucrative appointment as Warden of the Royal Mint set the seal on John's fortunes and established a royal connection which was to last until his son James' execution in 1573.

Appointments to the Royal Mint indicated both royal patronage to a particular goldsmith but also a relationship of trust, since the safety of the coinage lay in the hands of the Warden and his officers such as the Royal Assay. Goldsmiths favoured in this way may also have been propping up royal finances with loans and guarantees.

Little is known about the circumstances of the Mossman appointment but it did herald an even greater honour, as John Mossman was quickly commissioned to redesign the Scottish Crown and to make a new Crown Matrimonial for James' French Queen, Marie de Guise. No more prestigious project could befall a Scottish goldsmith for James wished to shine as a European Renaissance Prince and King of Scots[3].

The patriotic tone extended even to the gold which was to be mined on Crawford Muir. The Duchess of Lorraine, Marie de Guise's aunt, sent miners from France in 1540 to work under Mossman's supervision. At the same time she dispatched a master mason, John Roytell, to assist Marie and her new husband in raising the cultural prestige of the Scottish Court. These transactions reveal John Mossman as a man of European experience, eligible to join the circle of craftsmen, artists and musicians at the Stewart Court. This European connection, combined with loyalty to the royal house of Stewart, was to characterize Mossman ambitions for the next thirty years. Tangible evidence of this Renaissance achievement survives in the reconstructed Crown now on display in Edinburgh Castle, and in the architecture and decoration of the House on the Royal Mile.

Before departing from John Mossman's distinguished career, it is worth noting that after the disaster of Solway Moss and James' subsequent death in 1543 he was immediately reappointed as Keeper of the Mint and remained in office until 1557[4]. Unfortunately none of Mossman's handiwork can be definitely identified apart from the ambitious and impressive Scottish Crown. The Matrimonial Crown which he designed has not survived. Sometime in the early 1550s John's first wife Marion Harlaw (herself previously a widow) died and he married Isobel Dee. Although John had first married in 1529 and James was already in his early twenties, Mossman credit remained high on the marriage market even in late middle age!

To contemporary burgesses the marriage of James Mossman and Mariota Arres must have seemed a match made in heaven, and it was a carefully regulated affair. On 10 January 1555 Mariota formally inherited the House in the Netherbow along with her father's other properties. Immediately, with the consent of her guardians Alexander Mossman and George Littlejohn, Mariota leased the house to John Mossman and Isobel Dee. This move may already have formed part of a betrothal agreement but certainly prefigured the shape of things to come.

A full prenuptial contract between James Mossman, heir apparent to John, and his affianced wife Mariota Arres survives in the protocol book of the Edinburgh lawyer Alexander King. The circumstances of this contract are notable because of the amount of property involved and because of the special care taken with regard to 'the land or tenement on the north side of the High Street between the lands of the late William Lockhart on the west and north and a land of the late William Reidpath on the east' – the House in the Netherbow[5].

Later sasines affecting the other properties mentioned in this contract refer to occupiers or tenants; there is no reference to tenants in the Netherbow house or to liferent during James Mossman's lifetime. The detailed legal arrangements made now and on later occasions are clearly designed to secure unbroken family occupation of a house intended as both a prestigious residence and place of business.

The settlement of 1556 also includes provision for John Mossman and Isobel Dee through the liferent of the family property in Forresters' Wynd, and special financial arrangements for Isobel herself. The latter suggests that John Mossman may already have been ill and that the family were thinking ahead to his death, which occurred in 1558 when he was still Dean of the Guild and a Town Councillor. The mantle of the family's fortunes then passed from John to James but a smooth succession had been secured and in 1558 James became a burgess of Edinburgh by right of his father. It is in the context of this double event – James' marriage and his assumption of the family business – that the House which stands in the Netherbow today must be understood.

Writers on Edinburgh's Old Town have assumed since Victorian times that the House in the Netherbow, as presently constituted, was developed in stages, possibly from the core of a typical two-storey burgh house. Investigation in 1990–91 however revealed that the galleries and attics were all part of one integrated design and build[6]. The attractive frontages on the west and south sides, the spacious living quarters on the first and second floors, the booths and shops on ground level, the extensive cellars, and the additional attic and loft accommodation, form part of a coherent and impressive whole. Moreover the arrangement of the outside stairs and the two turnpike stairs, each with their forestairs or galleries, carefully preserves independent access to each part of the house, foreland and backland, so allowing for letting if necessary or for the convenient housing of relations, servants and apprentices.

On the west front the Mossman coat of arms, adapted with three gold crowns to represent the goldsmiths, is flanked by the initials JM and MA whether you read across or down. The correspondence between building and documentary record seems exact. A further record in the Register of the Privy Seal dated 12 May 1557 grants permission to James Mossman and Mariota Arres to build cellars for their house on the 'south side of the Hie Gate'. Royal permission was required for any encroachment on public space in a royal burgh and this entry shows not only that James and Mariota were simultaneously developing another property for let, but that their property on the north side already possessed cellars. The rebuilding of the Netherbow house, incorporating foreland and backland into an outstanding town residence, was the centrepiece of a concerted financial strategy.

Even more significant than the internal lay-out is the style and ornamentation of James and Mariota's frontage. Continental influence is marked in the classically correct Doric pilasters framing the first-floor window and in the decorative urns and garlands. Continuous masonry construction ties the ashlar frontage into the remarkably delicate piers which support the south wall and provide a sixteenth century shopping arcade with sheltered access to booths and cellars.[7] The Netherbow house is a very early, if not the earliest, Scottish example of the adaptation of the Renaissance style to Northern European domestic architecture.

The same mixing of styles is apparent in the house's remarkable external ornamentation or iconography. In addition to the Mossman coat of arms, there is a Biblical motto, a sundial and a figure in three-quarters relief, all handsomely carved in stone. The text in Scots – 'Luve God abuve al and yi nychtbour as yersel' – is a northern vernacular element and one of the earliest of the carved texts which are a notable feature of Edinburgh's Old Town. The sundial however embodies a strand of Renaissance thinking that originated in Italy but reached Scotland through France. Beneath the dial Moses is portrayed receiving the revelation of the law on Sinai, but in this case he is also a divine philosopher – the Hebraic Plato – gazing towards the Sun which is the light of God and of Reason. To emphasise this universality, God is named in Greek, Latin and English. The combination of this Old Testament vision with the Biblical text which provides Christ's own summary of the Law underpins this universality by linking the Old and New Testaments in an integrated revelation.

The blending of the Classical and the Biblical is clearly pre-Reformation and indicative of the Francophile Scottish Court rather than the religion of John Knox. Together text and symbol present a broad interpretation of religion, uniting the Old and New Testaments in the stream of contemporary Christian Humanism.

At the time that Mossman's house was conceived and built, work was also being carried out at Holyrood Palace (using the same Craigmillar stone) by John Roytell, the master mason who had reached Scotland in 1543 in the same ship as John Mossman's French miners. Roytell was, like the Mossmans, a loyal servant of the Scottish Court heavily dependent on royal patronage. He was made a burgess of Edinburgh at the request of the Abbot of Holyrood in 1550 and was confirmed as Principal Master Mason for life in 1557. Further up the High Street he was responsible for Marie de Guise's house in the Lawnmarket. It was to Roytell that Mossman surely turned in 1556–57 to stamp a distinctive courtly character on the residence of the royal goldsmiths.[8] The French Renaissance style and the fine workmanship of the west façade are evidence of his direct supervision, contrasting with the more traditional corbels of the same date on the south side. Lesser details would be left to native craftsmen at an appropriately cheaper rate.

Rarely can a young burgess couple have entered on marriage with such auspicious auguries. As James and Mariota moved in in 1558 it must have seemed as if the Mossmans were at the apogee of their fortunes. In fact the see-saw of history would take them both higher in future and much much lower.

NOTES

1. See *First Minute Book, 1525–1738*, the Incorporation of Goldsmiths of the City of Edinburgh.
2. *Register of the Privy Seal of Scotland*, 24 August 1539.
3. See C.J. Burnet and C.J. Tabraham, *The Honours of Scotland* (Edinburgh 1993).
4. *Register of the Privy Seal of Scotland*, 1 March 1543 and 9 November 1557.
5. *Protocol Book of Alexander King*, 27 July 1556.
6. See D. Smith and Benjamin Tindall Architects, *John Knox House, Interim Report to The Edinburgh Old Town Committee for Conservation and Renewal* (Edinburgh, 1991).
7. *Ibid.*
8. *Ibid.* See also the detailed Survey Drawings of John Knox House (1990) by Benjamin Tindall Architects lodged with the National Monuments Record.

CHAPTER FOUR

IN TIME OF STRIFE

In 1557 there was little sign of the upheavals which were to rock Scotland over the next three years and leave the body politic subject to conflict and instability until the 1580s. In fact, the worst crisis of religion seemed to be over. After the advance of the Lutheran 'heresy' in the 1540s Protestantism had apparently been contained and an alternative programme of orthodox Catholic reform was underway. At the same time the Queen Regent, Marie de Guise, had not entirely closed the door on the new religious ideas, allowing some toleration in the interests of national stability and unity.

Marie de Guise is one of Scotland's better royal rulers, who in the face of adverse circumstances held the country together and secured the succession of her daughter to the Scottish Crown in her own right without subordination to any foreign power. She also maintained stable government in Scotland which was only disrupted at the end of her reign by circumstances outwith her control. The Mossmans were loyal servants of the Regency and on 9 November 1557 they received their reward when Walter Mossman, James' brother, succeeded his father as Keeper of the Royal Mint.[1] But by 1559 Marie de Guise was dead, her government was dissolved and the Mossmans ousted from Court office. The Protestant Reformation had begun.

One of the puzzles of the Reformation is the rapidity and relative ease with which one of the most fundamental shifts in Scottish national life took place between 1558 and 1560. Another is the extent to which John Knox was really the decisive leader of these events or merely one of their instruments.

The two questions are closely connected since Knox's own account in his *Historie of the Reformation* has been universally influential and even seductive in later views of the troubles in Scotland. Not only does Knox place himself at the centre of events with linguistic verve and dramatic gusto, but he presents the conflict as a clash between black and white – the true believers versus corrupt Papists and timid compromisers. In Knox's account there is no place for people like the Mossmans who remained honourably loyal to the old regime. The reality may have been more complex.

The really decisive steps were taken by a minority of the Scottish nobility – the Lords of the Congregation – acting from a mixture of religious and political motives. As events unfolded they gathered the support of other great magnates and of a majority of the laird or gentry class whose economic rise had largely been at the expense of the Church's traditional landholdings. In the burghs more forces were brought into play as popular resentment at the wealth and privileges of the Church combined with a leaven of convinced Protestantism to attack the fabric of Catholicism. By and large the Town Councils – Merchants and Craftsmen – temporized, swinging ultimately behind the new order because it increasingly offered the best chance of stability and security.

It was this complex coalition which came together in the Reformation Parliament of 1560 which met without royal approval to reject the authority of the Pope over the Scottish Church, to proscribe the saying of the Mass, and to approve a Reformed Confession of Faith. As a co-author of the Scots Confession and the newly appointed minister of St Giles Church in Edinburgh, Knox was an articulate spokesman for the new agenda. But the same coalition of forces was not prepared to deny the role of royal authority in the government of the new Kirk, or to support the radical blueprint for social change (for a reformed and godly society) contained in the First Book of Discipline, also co-authored by Knox. This manifesto was approved by the General Assembly of the new Kirk but never accepted by Parliament. Knox's position as a radical Calvinist in the 1560s was composed as much of weakness as of strength, and it is against this background that we must understand many of the fulminations in the *Historie*, and in particular the harshness of his opposition to Mary Queen of Scots.

It was to the return of Mary from France that many in Scotland, including the Mossmans, looked for a return to stability, and they were not entirely disappointed. Following negotiations with Lord James Stewart, Mary's half-brother and leader of the Protestant Lords, Mary returned in August 1561 guaranteed, despite Knox's bitter opposition, the practice of the Catholic faith within her private chapel. In October 1561 James Mossman celebrated by installing new carved panelling in the principal room of the House in the Netherbow, complete with a lion rampant and the date 31 October 1561 – All Hallows Eve. A general restoration of the good old ways seemed in sight but Mossman had particular reasons for celebration since on 8 November 1561 the Register of the Privy Seal of Scotland formally records his appointment as Master Assayer of the Royal Mint.[2] Though the job of Warden remained in the hands of the Protestant appointee of 1559, this was clearly, within political limitations, a small step towards the reestablishment of the royal ascendancy. Perhaps the old religion would soon also be restored.

Mary brought a new lustre to the Scottish Court along with the glamour of a European Renaissance reputation. Between 1561 and 1566 the Queen's apartments at Holyrood were refurbished in the continental style and the fine arts were once again patronized. During these five years several payments to James Mossman are recorded in the Queen's household accounts. Unfortunately no specific piece of jewellery has been identified as Mossman's work but, like his father before him, the royal goldsmith was clearly a loyal and favoured servant of the Crown. The relationship was sealed when in 1565 James was knighted by the young Queen, becoming Sir James Mossman, Royal Assay. The House in the Netherbow identified with the Palace and followed its fashions, albeit on a more modest scale.

Despite this courtly renaissance, storm clouds gathered. Notwithstanding her attempt to settle the vexed question of Church finances, Mary's relationship with the Protestant Kirk went from bad to worse, at a time when the Kirk was consolidating its position particularly in the burghs. The mere existence of a Catholic Court was both galling and threatening to Knox who maintained a virulent campaign against Mary. The young Queen was more successful at first in dealing with the Scots magnates whose support was essential to her rule, but these gains were dissipated by the misjudgement of Mary's first marriage to Henry Darnley and the disaster of her second to the able but politically isolated Earl of Bothwell. Finally Mary capped a catalogue of mistakes by fleeing to England after the Battle of Langside leaving her supporters (potentially still the majority) without leadership. The welcome awaiting Mary at the hands of her royal cousin of England, the politically astute Elizabeth, is too well known to require repetition.

Yet despite these errors Scotland retained a natural political bias in favour of legitimate royal authority, if reasonably exercised. The 'Queen's Men' were the expression of this standpoint, opposing the forced abdication of Mary which had been engineered in 1567 by Lord James. In 1568 Sir William Kirkcaldy of Grange, the Protestant Governor of Edinburgh Castle, declared his support for Mary and held the Castle for the Queen's Men. In the same year James Mossman was a member of the Town Council in his own right rather than as Deacon of the Goldsmith's Guild. A majority of the Council, under the loyalist Provost Sir Simon Preston of Craigmillar, sided with Mary and backed Kirkcaldy of Grange.

In some ways the events of 1568 to 1573, when Edinburgh Castle finally surrendered to the Protestant Government, were a more serious threat to Scotland than the 'revolution' of 1558–60, since it involved a dispute about the legitimacy and possession of the Crown, that central symbol of authority and stability. In addition, from 1571 when the Castle was seriously besieged, the physical effects on Edinburgh were worse than anything that had happened since the destruction at English hands in 1544.

The only consolation was that, until the long requested arrival of English military technology to blast the castle into surrender, foreign intervention was not an immediate risk and the real damage was all self-inflicted.

This was a dispute which cut across lines of religion and even divided families. James Mossman's younger brother John, who had become a Protestant, supported the King's Men[3]. He was also a goldsmith and it was his line of the family that designed some of the earliest Scottish Communion Cups[4]. For James by contrast there can have been little option but to maintain his support for Mary since for two generations the family fortunes had been closely linked to the Court. But this was not just an issue of self-interest. There is no surviving documentary evidence to reveal Mossman's feelings but the house which embodies his values and aspirations speaks eloquently of his wholehearted identification with the culture and religion of Scotland's Renaissance Queen. Emotional loyalty must have undergirded this relationship.

Whether James hesitated in his commitment is unknown but there is some evidence to suggest anxiety. On 26 July 1568, James and Mariota transferred ownership of the family house to their eldest son John who was still a minor.[5] As normal in these cases the liferent of the property was vested in the parents, but less normally an·option of buying back the house was left open. It is hard not to read this as a precautionary measure, ahead of the customary generational settlement, against the threat posed to James by the political situation. Even as late as September 1570 James and Mariota are sinking some of their disposable income in that most secure of all 16th century assets land, adding ground in Currie to their existing holdings in Edinburgh and Linlithgow.[6]

By this time Sir James Mossman was a notable supporter of the garrison in Edinburgh Castle and was soon to be the organiser of a 'cunyie' or Mint in the fortress which effectively financed the Marian party. For the Royal Assay this was the most practical and significant support possible. To the Protestant government this was treason and counterfeiting – both of them capital crimes. But even as this crisis was still developing, late in 1570, Mariota died.

Whether Mariota had been ill for some time is unknown. Certainly this would lend extra point to the transfer of 1568 since Mariota was by the terms of her marriage settlement joint owner of the family home. Similarly the land purchase could be read as a canny anticipation of death. Whatever the background, public and private events conspired to provoke a crisis in family affairs. James' response was to maintain his staunch support for the Queen's cause and to marry again, within a few months of Mariota's death.

Remarriage following the death of a spouse was a common occurrence in 16th century Scotland. James' father John had been married twice, and John Knox married a 17 year old aristocrat after the death of his first wife. Significantly contemporaries criticised the Reformer for reaching above himself socially rather than for marrying someone thirty years younger. James' new bride was Janet King, daughter of the prominent Edinburgh notary Alexander King. She was still alive in 1600 and must have been at least twenty years the goldsmith's junior. The really interesting thing about this marriage however is not the age differential but the fact that in February 1571 Mossman's wealth and social position made him eminently marriageable despite the crisis in national affairs, not least in Edinburgh. The remarriage is testimony to the fact that marriage and property remained key preoccupations in a burgh society which had lived through many national crises. In addition the cause of the Queen's Men was seen as legitimate, respectable and still potentially successful.

The new turn of events is once again mirrored in the fate of the Netherbow house since on 23 February 1571 James took up the option of buying back the property which had technically been transferred to his son John, transferring it anew to the joint ownership of himself and Janet King[7]. This move gave Janet the same security which Mariota had previously enjoyed through her joint ownership of the house. It had now become a provision for Janet in the likely event of James dying first.

James however did not have much time to relish his newly wedded state since public affairs took a turn for the worse. The Earl of Morton, now Protestant Regent, began in earnest to besiege Edinburgh Castle. In May 1571 John Knox had to leave for the safety of St Andrews since the upper half of the town became dangerously embroiled in the conflict with even the tower of St Giles commandeered as a firing post. This was now a real civil war fought out at Edinburgh's expense. James Mossman and his brother-in-law James Cockie and their wives took refuge in the Castle, under the leadership of Kirkcaldy of Grange.

NOTES

1. *Register of the Privy Seal of Scotland*, 9 November 1557
2. The Master Assayer was responsible for maintaining the correct balance of precious and base metals in the coinage.
3. See M. Lynch *Edinburgh and the Reformation* (Edinburgh, 1981), p. 305.
4. The Roseneath Cups are held separately in the National Museums of Scotland and the Huntly House Museum, Canongate, Edinburgh.
5. *Protocol Book of Alexander Guthrie*, 26 July 1568.
6. *Register of the Great Seal of Scotland*, 30 September 1570.
7. *Protocol Book of Alexander Guthrie*, 23 February 1571.

CHAPTER FIVE

DECLINE AND FALL

Between 1571 and 1573 events conspired against the Queen's Men and the garrison of Edinburgh Castle. The leadership of the Scottish government passed from the ineffective Earls of Lennox and then Mar to the very determined Earl of Morton. English support to the King's Men was increased and a string of notable magnates defected to the government cause. In 1572 the burgh of Edinburgh was occupied and the besiegers' grip on the castle tightened. Nonetheless under the inspiring generalship of Kirkcaldy of Grange the Marians refused to surrender.

Even in 1571 life in Edinburgh must have gone on much as normal, despite the nearby presence of a hostile army and bursts of activity such as the ineffectual attack on the castle in October. The goldsmith's shop in the Netherbow would still be open and there was nothing to prevent James Mossman and Janet King enjoying the first months of marriage in their own home. John Knox's withdrawal to St Andrew's in May 1571 is clear evidence that the town was under the control of the Queen's Men. By early 1572 however many of the Marians had taken up residence in the castle itself and the government of the King's Men was progressively strengthening its position.

On 24 April 1572, James Mossman was formally dismissed from his post as Royal Assay. The Register of the Privy Seal records the appointment of Thomas Acheson as

> Master Assayer of his grace's cunye and money in succesion to James Mossman, who has not only ceased from the said office but has conveyed himself within the Castle of Edinburgh and there remains with our sovereign lord's rebels and declared traitors, devising and forging false and counterfeit cunye within the same.[1]

On 29 June 1572 Mossman was outlawed – 'put to the horn' – and his goods made forfeit.[2] On the same day the Register records the award of Mossman's confiscated goods or movable property to a Captain Walter Aikman in the besieging army. These are valuable sources which throw light on a unique episode in the history of the Scottish Mint and on the most controversial few months in the history of the House in the Netherbow.

On 12 March 1572 and again in early April, the Diurnal of Remarkable Occurents, a contemporary chronicle written in Edinburgh, refers to the creation of a cunyiehous or Mint in the castle and describes the coinage it produced.[3] In June 1572 Lord Burghley at Elizabeth's Court in England received a sample of the coins. On 30th June, a two-month truce was signed and its terms included a promise to cease coining in the castle, but in August the Earl of Mar asserted that counterfeiting had continued in the castle since the truce. The same accusation was made during a further truce which began on 8 October.

Counterfeiting was an extremely serious offence in the 16th century since the purity of the coinage was the guarantee of economic stability, while the operation of the Mint was a profitable source of government revenue. Coining required specialist skills and the setting up of a rival Marian Mint depended on the expertise of Mossman and his relation James Cockie who, as a skilled engraver, produced the punches and dies. The Diurnal's March date for the start of the operation is confirmed by the Register of the Privy Seal: in March 1572 James Mossman was still receiving payment as the Royal Assay, but by April he was officially a traitor, 'put to the horn', and his goods forfeit. In the judgement of Joan Murray, who has made a special study of the Marian coinage, the two goldsmiths 'could hardly fail to realise that they were risking everything by coining for the Marians at a time when that party was already on the decline'. Very few of the Marian coins have been certainly identified for they were not the work of common counterfeiters but of recognised experts.[4]

The valuable record of the Privy Seal also has some bearing on the vexed question of whether John Knox ever lived in the House in the Netherbow which has been known for two centuries by his name. It has often been suggested that Knox lived in Mossman's house when he returned from St Andrews on 31 July 1572 until his death on 24 November. Certainly any occupation of the House in the Netherbow by Knox before this date is highly unlikely. It has however equally been argued that any stay by Knox during this period is impossible since Mossman would have returned to his own home during the successive truces negotiated that summer and autumn between the castle garrison and its besiegers[5]

The evidence of the Register, including the confiscation of Mossman's goods, does not support a scenario in which Mossman could have returned freely to his house and resumed business under the terms of the truce. In addition there is the further evidence that coining continued in the castle during the truce. Mossman was no ordinary member of the garrison but the architect of its financial fortunes closely associated with the very sensitive issue of the Mint. It seems likely that he remained in the castle, probably with his wife, during the truces, while his property in the town was subject to the government decrees made before the first truce was declared. The House in the Netherbow – one of the finest on the High Street – may therefore have been empty. Moreover it is conveniently situated within clear sight of St Giles Church, though out of military danger.

On the other hand there is no positive sixteenth century evidence to link Knox with Mossman's house. On present knowledge Knox's possible residence in the house during the last months of his life can neither be proved nor disproved. In fact the whole issue has distracted attention from what can be reliably established about the fate of the house and its owners. That story is all too clear in terms which are spelled out by that most authentic of sources, the Register of the Privy Seal of Scotland and the Register of the Great Seal.

On 14 March 1573, as the siege continued, the Register records the legitimisation of the three illegitimate children of Captain Walter Aikman, now deceased, and Marion Pott. The purpose of this move is to enable Aikman's children to inherit the goods confiscated from James Mossman. A whole story is contained in a few lines. The official effort suggests that Aikman died in action. Marion Pott was a common law wife and possibly a camp follower. The need for this further decree may be purely legal but does suggest that the confiscated goods had not yet been secured because they were in the castle. These however are incidentals since the Register's main thrust is remorselessly vivid.

Gift to the same of the escheat of the goods of James Mossman, goldsmith burgess of Edinburgh, become in will fugitive or at the horn for taking part with Sir William Kirkcaldy sometime of Grange,

William Maitland younger, sometime of Lethington, and other declared traitors in holding the Burgh and Castle of Edinburgh against the King, furnishing them with victuals and otherwise intercommuning with them, coming to the fields with displayed banners against the King's authority, slaughter and mutilation of faithful lieges.[6]

A further irritation, unmentioned by the Register, was the garrison's possession of the Scottish Crown Jewels, without which Parliament could not legally convene since the regalia symbolized the royal presence. In this regard at least Mossman was custodian of his own father's handiwork.

A heavier blow was reserved for 2 May 1573 when the Register of the Great Seal records the gift to John Carmichael of Carmichael, captain of a hundred light horse in the government army, of Sir James Mossman's property.[7] The list contains all the houses mentioned in James and Mariota's marriage settlement of 1556, including the family house in the Netherbow, and the landholdings in Linlithgow and Currie. The basis of the Mossman's prosperity was cut away at a single stroke of the judicial pen. Such were the penalties of treason or loyalty, depending on your perspective.

John Carmichael the younger was a Douglas and a Morton loyalist. His father was married to a half-sister of the Earl of Morton and another Douglas relation, George Douglas of Parkhead, was to become Captain of Edinburgh Castle and Provost of Edinburgh after the defeat of the Marians. As Regent of Scotland the Earl of Morton was a ruthless nepotist, rewarding his kinsmen with property and offices. Carmichael himself was primarily a soldier and later in his career was appointed Keeper of Liddesdale in the troubled Borders. The award of the Mossman property was a recognition of Carmichael's role in the siege, including the recruitment and upkeep of his cavalry squadron.[8]

Within a month, on 28 May 1573, the castle fell, pounded into submission by a battery of English cannon transported north specially for the job. Reprisals were deliberately restrained with an emphasis on fines rather than imprisonment or execution. But even before the castle's fall, a few key figures had been selected for trial. Notable among these were Kirkcaldy of Grange the commander and Mary's one-time secretary Maitland of Lethington, who seems to have anticipated the result by taking poison. Also included were Sir James Mossman and James Cockie – the 'counterfeiters'.

The result was a foregone conclusion and the *Diurnal of Occurents* has an eyewitness flavour when it notes that on 3 August 1573 Kirkcaldy of Grange, Mossman and Cockie were 'harled in two carts backward from the Abbey to the Cross' and hanged. The route from Holyrood to the Mercat Cross passes within touching distance of the House in the Netherbow, symbol of all Mossman's ambitions and achievements in his public and personal life. The Register is less vivid but equally blunt, recording that the two goldsmiths were 'hangit on the 3rd of August and their heads put up upon the castle wall'. The charge was treason.

A compelling anecdote preserved by Thomas Smeton links John Knox's illness and death with the final fate of his erstwhile ally Kirkcaldy of Grange. 'Go', the dying Reformer is reputed to have said, to David Lindesay the Minister of Leith 'go to yonder man in the castle – he whom ye know I have loved so dearly – tell him that I have sent ye once more to warn him, in the name of God, to leave that evil cause, for neither the craigy rock in which he so miserably confides, nor the carnal prudence of that man Lethington, whom he esteems even as a demi-god, nor the assistance of strangers, shall preserve him; but he shall be disgracefully dragged forth to punishment and hanged on a gallows in the face of the sun, unless he speedily amend his life, and flee to the mercy of God.' Having spurned this prophecy Kirkcaldy is supposed to have remembered it on the day of his execution.[9]

The fate of Kirkcaldy of Grange and his associates was long remembered in Edinburgh and the defence of the castle celebrated as a gallant if ultimately hopeless act. Kirkcaldy's role is commemorated in a magnificent memorial placed on the inner wall of the castle, clearly visible on the main visitor route. Mossman's part is largely forgotten though the Trades Banner or 'Blue Blanket' of Edinburgh, whose predecessor hung in the goldsmith's chapel in St Giles' Church, still bears words which could stand as his epitaph: 'we that is tradds shall ever pray to be faithful for the defence of his sacred majesties royal persone till death'.[10]

For the Mossman goldsmiths the blow was considerable. Mariota's children were left without a father while Janet had a baby daughter to consider. Apart from the personal tragedy the family's standing and prestige never recovered from this setback. Gradually some of the family property was bought back with provision being made for Janet King through repurchase of the House in the

Netherbow. It was not uncommon for confiscated property to be recouped in this way and the young widow had some moral if not a legal claim to the rights assigned in her marriage settlement. The date of these transactions has not yet been ascertained but with the thoroughgoing defeat of the Marians the climate was conciliatory and the House may have been recovered relatively quickly. In 1581 Janet was confirmed in her ownership of the lands in Linlithgow and in 1592 the Currie holdings were also regained.[11]

Re-establishing the family fortunes was however far from painless as a remarkable letter from James' son John Mossman to Mary Queen of Scots demonstrates. It appears from this letter to the imprisoned Mary, dated 12 November 1582, that John had been in London for four months pressing a suit for financial assistance to set him up in a trade so that he could provide for his orphaned brothers and sisters. The Calendar of State Papers quotes and transliterates as follows:

"Unto zour grace and majestie maist excellant quhome God mott presarve in lange lyfe and guid halthe"; this present letter of supplication directed unto your majesty is to call your highness to remembrance of me, John Mosman, your grace's true and faithful subject, "quhome had my father James Mosman, goldsmyth, put to daithe and schamfullie excecutit weithe the Lerd of Grange," and all because he was your grace's master coiner and true subject. Therefore, seeing your grace rewards sundry others who have not done such good service to your highness as he did, and leaving so many poor fatherless bairns behind him, who have no support but of God and of your grace, by decease of their father in your highness's true service, "for the liefe of Almechtie God that it vill plese zour majestie to consyder the saming and to gef me ane certene certane [sic] sume to make me ane tred or stoile to support the pure orpheillenes quhome prayis dayle for your majestie," and hoping for your support and aid. I have been here in London this four month, abiding continually upon your grace's answer and goodwill, "and to zit can gat none, and hes spend all that I had, abidyng upone the saming quhan God sould mowe zour gracis hart; thairfor for Godes cause to vyrt to the Franche ambassatour Monsiuer Movesser to ansuer me of that . . . quhilk zour henes is villing to allow upone me and the rest of my pour brether and sesteres; because I have nocht ane panay to spend I have bodin heir so lang forder." I sent "ane compt" to your grace "unto zour henes," whereby your majesty was "adatit" to my father; but I refer all to your grace's goodwill and discretion, which I doubt not but your grace will consider "the saming."

I would write to your highness of sundry things, "bot I take feir and dar nocht vryte as I vald, thairfoir appardone me." If it may please your majesty to send any letters to Scotland or to France or "uther quhair," employ me as one "quhome to" your majesty may give credit, and [I] will venture my life to do my duty therein London. *Signed* "Jhone Mosman, zounger."[12]

There is no evidence that John's suit was successful or that his father's loyalty was repaid, but John did not return to the family trade of goldsmith and is described in later documents as John Mossman, Merchant. Also interesting in this letter is John's continuing willingness to serve the Marian cause.

During the same period the Mossman tradition of goldsmithing was continued through James' younger brother John Mossman who had become a Protestant at the time of the Reformation in 1559-60. Among John's productions are the outstanding early examples of Protestant communion ware, the Roseneath Cups. These silver cups are the only definitely ascribed Mossman artefact to survive apart from the Scottish Crown. This is particularly frustrating since the Calendar of State Papers contains a detailed description of the royal jewels which were held in the castle along with the crown and sceptre.

"Memor of the Kingis Jewellis now being in the Marschell of Barwickes handes."

Certain buttons of gold with rubies, in weight 2 lbs. 6 ounces. "Off garnissingis contenand of wecht twa pund five unces," and "garnissing" containing eleven "diamantes," whereof there is a great diamond "tailzeit," and certain pearls. Nine great rubies and forty great pearls. "Thir peces being liand in wed to diverse wer brocht to Leith to Grange, he then being in the Marschellis handes, and be him deliverit to the Marschell."

A "garnissing" of diamonds "esmailled" with black, containing sixteen diamonds, and sixteen roses of gold between. A less "garnissing" containing 18 diamonds, and 19 roses of gold between. A "carcan" containing 13 diamonds and 13 roses of gold. These pieces were delivered to the Marshal of Berwick by Mr. Archibald Dowglas.

Ten diamonds or "quheit saphires" set in gold with 11 "knoppis" of gold between. A belt of roses, diamonds, and pearls, "ilkane contenand ten or xx cordelires of gold betwene." "Thre great rubyes of ajoin and a perll of ilkane of thame." A "hingar" of a belt of pearl containing eleven knots, with three pearls in each one of them, and eleven "cordeleris" with

14 pearls in each one of them, with a "hupe" at the end thereof. A "hingand" saphire set in gold, and a great pearl at the end of it. Another saphire ajoining. Three diamonds and three rubies. 18 knots of pearls set in gold, with "twa perlis in ilkane of thame." A chain of pearls with two "rankes" of pearls and 24 "markes" of little diamonds and small rubies in gold, "ten perlis betwene everilk mark." A "garnissing" containing 9 roses of rubies and ten "knoppes" of pearls with a pearl "hingand" at each ruby. A pair of bracelets of gold "of musk," each bracelet containing four pieces, and in every piece 8 diamonds and 7 rubies, and 11 pearls in them both. "Twa quaiffis, ane collair, and ane pair of sleves of perll." Five great saphires set in gold. A carcan of saphires and pearls. "Thir peces being in the handes of umqwhile James Mosman laid in wed to him be Grange for certane sowmes of money, wer agane deliverit be the said Mosman to Grange the day of the randering of the castell, and being thairefter placit be Grange in a coffer within his chalmer quhair he lay in the castell, the same coffer and peces of jewellis become in the Marschell of Barwickis handes."[13]

Some of these items must have been the handiwork of the two generations of Mossman royal goldsmiths. The ultimate fate of this war booty is unknown, but their value reflects the extraordinary extent to which James Mossman was financing the defence of Edinburgh Castle with his own money — finance for which the royal jewels were surety.

One last curious footnote to the dispersion and partial recovery of James Mossman's estate was uncovered in 1990 when a detailed examination was undertaken of the House in the Netherbow. On the ground floor, beneath a later ceiling, the gaps between the 16th century timbers were plastered over with the pages of 16th century printed books, representing a range of European Renaissance works. Among these printed items was one handwritten fragment in which the name Kirkcaldy of Grange is clearly legible.[14] Fortunately another aspect of Mossman's legacy, the house itself, has survived the vicissitudes of four centuries in rather better shape than what may be the fragmentary remains of the royal goldsmith's books and papers.

NOTES

1. *Register of the Privy Seal of Scotland*, 24 April 1572.
2. *Register of the Privy Seal of Scotland*, 29 June 1572.

3. See T. Thomson (ed.) *A Diurnal of Remarkable Occurrents* (Edinburgh, 1833) and J.E.L. Murray 'The Coinage of the Marians in Edinburgh Castle in 1572' in *The British Numismatic Journal*, vol. 57, 1987.
4. *Ibid.*
5. See R. Miller, *John Knox and the Town Council of Edinburgh* (Edinburgh, 1898).
6. *Register of the Privy Seal of Scotland*, 14 March 1573.
7. *Register of the Great Seal of Scotland*, 2 May 1573.
8. See G. R. Hewitt, *Scotland under Morton 1572–80* (Edinburgh, 1982), pp. 36–37 and p. 130.
9. See D. Laing (ed.), *The Works of John Knox* (Edinburgh, 1864), vol. vi. pp. 634–44 for Thomas Smeton's retrospective account of these events.
10. The oldest surviving 'Blue Blanket' is preserved in the care of the Incorporated Trades of Edinburgh at the Trades Maiden Hospital.
11. T. Thomson and C. Innes (eds.) *The Acts of the Parliament of Scotland 1124–1707*, (Edinburgh, 1814-75), vol. III, June 20 1581.
12. J. Bain and others (eds.) *Calendar of State Papers relating to Scotland and Mary Queen of Scots* (London, 1898-1969) 211 p. 210, November 12 1582.
13. *Ibid.* 690 p.584, June 13 1573.
14. Deposited in the National Library of Scotland: Knox House MS Fragment.

CHAPTER SIX

HIGH STREET HOUSES

When Walter Reidpath, John Arres and then James Mossman made the area around the Netherbow Port the focus of their business it was not a heavily built up area, except on the High Street and beside the gate. It was the upmarket end of town, a kind of garden suburb in which the wealthy maintained town houses on the open ground to the north and south of the main thoroughfare. Mossman's reconstituted residence of 1557 would not therefore have seemed out of place, though it was designed on the High Street as a place of trade and commerce.

In the second half of the 16th century and even more in the 17th, the Netherbow area became built up as the garden ground was filled with new houses. This resulted in continuous rows of buildings at right angles to the High Street separated only by the resultant closes and interspersed courtyards. In addition multi-occupancy of houses became the norm as those who could afford space and privacy moved outside the walls into areas such as the Burgh of the Canongate.

The way in which the usage of the House in the Netherbow changed during this period can be paralleled in the history of houses of a similar age, such as Henry Cant's tenement in Advocates' Close.[1] But the story of the Netherbow building has the additional merit of continuity since the link between the Mossman family and its erstwhile mansion was sustained through these decades.

As indicated in the previous chapter, the date by which Janet King, through the good offices of her stepson John, regained her rights over the family house is unknown, but the use to which she put her widow's portion can be traced in the detailed daily records of the Edinburgh notaries. The fullest picture is in fact a retrospect, because on 22 May 1600 Janet Mossman finally divided up the House in the Netherbow in the interests of her family and her tenants. Presumably this was a conventional settlement of her affairs in the face of old age and death, but Janet herself was there on the day along with the notary Alexander Guthrie, Sarah the wife of her loyal stepson, and her own daughter, another Janet, who was now Mrs Oswald. Several witnesses were also convened to testify to the serious business of the day.[2]

The division of 22 May 1600 confirms the current usage of the property while passing the ownership of some parts to the family and others to the tenants. The resulting list makes interesting reading, beginning from the cellars or laigh floor.

OCCUPATION OF THE HOUSE IN THE NETHERBOW
MAY 1600

1	Laigh Floor:	Three Cellars	Andrew Smyth, Spurrier
		Fore Cellar	The Widow Stevenson
		Nether Cellar	John Hutchinson
2	Ground Floor:	House of Hall and two Chambers	Murdoch Brown, Bonnetmaker
		Main Shop or Merchant's Booth	John Baxter, Tailor
		Stane Shop on west side	James Maistertoun Merchant
		Forebooth on south side	Murdoch Brown, Bonnetmaker
		Penteis or lean-to booth, below outside stairs	Murdoch Brown, Bonnetmaker
3	First Floor:	House of Large Hall and two Chambers	John Baxter, Tailor
4	Second Floor:	Principal Dwelling House of Hall and two Forestairs (landings or galleries)	Lady Johnson
		Back House of single Chamber	John Henderson
5	Third Floor:	Last Dwelling House of Hall, Chamber and Loftroom above the turnpike.	Captain Davidson

The first thing to be said about these dispositions is that they correspond in close detail to the House in the Netherbow as it exists today, with the exception of the second chamber in John

Baxter's first floor house which was demolished in the late 19th century, and John Hutchinson's nether cellar which is now filled in. Otherwise the pattern is complete so affirming the integrity of the present building and its continuity from the Mossman period.

Other interesting conclusions can however be garnered from this information. The multiple usage of the cellars and booths by different trades probably formed part of James Mossman's original scheme for the property. Now however there is a spread of social classes among the residents from the aristocratic Lady Johnson (a Douglas and perhaps a relic of John Carmichael's interest?), through a retired military gentleman and the substantial tradesmen, to the nondescript John Henderson with his one room and the unfortunate Widow Stevenson in her single cellar. In the course of the 17th century Edinburgh was to become famous for this vertical form of 'democratic' hierarchy which became more elongated as the buildings became higher.

A second interesting feature of the list is that Murdoch Brown on the ground floor and John Baxter on the first floor have breached the old division between foreland and backland by uniting rooms in both. Baxter in particular occupies a complete level. This establishes a trend which was to continue in the 17th century until each floor provided one logical holding.

This necessitated an opening on each floor in the massive central wall (originally the joint gable), despite the increasing disparity of levels the higher up the building one climbs. By the middle of the century the original vertical division had been entirely superseded though unless it is kept in mind the present layout of the house with its double provision of galleries and stairs makes no sense.

Until 22 May 1600 the whole complex remained the property of Janet King and her daughter Janet Mossman or Oswald, but the transactions on that day finally broke up the Mossman inheritance by ownership as well as occupation.

OWNERSHIP OF THE HOUSE IN THE NETHERBOW AS FROM 22 MAY 1600

1   Laigh Floor:
     Three Cellars occupied by Smyth the Spurrier transferred from Janet King and Janet Mossman to the ownership of John Mossman and then on the same day to John Baxter the Tailor.

Fore Cellar beneath the main shop, occupied by Widow Stevenson, transferred from Janet King and Janet Mossman to John Baxter and then to his wife Agnes Chalmers.

Nether Cellar transferred from Janet King and Janet Mossman to Humphrey Carwood and his wife Agnes Wilkie.

2   Ground Floor:
House of Hall and two Chambers, occupied by Murdoch Brown the Bonnetmaker, transferred from Janet King and Janet Mossman to John Mossman, his wife Sarah Abercrombie and his son John Mossman.

Stone Shope on the west side, occupied by John Maistertoun the Merchant, transferred from Janet King and Janet Mossman to John Mossman, Sarah Abercrombie and John Mossman, with rental assigned to Captain John Davidson.

Main Shop or Merchant's Booth, occupied by John Baxter, transferred from Janet King and Janet Mossman to John Baxter and then to his wife Agnes Chalmers.

Forebooth on south side, occupied by Murdoch Brown the Bonnetmaker, transferred from Janet King and Janet Mossman to Humphrey Carwood and Agnes Wilkie.

Penteis or lean-to booth below the outside stairs, occupied by Murdoch Brown the Bonnetmaker, transferred from Janet King and Janet Mossman to Humphrey Carwood and Agnes Wilkie.

3   First Floor:
House of Large Hall and two Chambers, occupied by Baxter the Tailor, transferred from Janet King and Janet Mossman to John Baxter and then to his wife Agnes Chalmers.

4   Second Floor:
Principal Dwelling House and two Forestairs, occupied by Lady Johnson, transferred from Janet King and Janet Mossman to Humphrey Carwood and his wife Agnes Wilkie.

Back House of a single Chamber, occupied by John Henderson, transferred from Janet King and Janet Mossman to Humphrey Carwood and Agnes Wilkie.

5   Third Floor:
Last Dwelling House of Hall, Chamber and Loftroom, occupied

by Captain John Davidson, transferred from Janet King and
Janet Mossman to Captain Davidson.

What is notable about these detailed arrangements, apart from
the work generated for the notary, is their stability. Sitting tenants
had the 'right to buy', while other owners took possession on the
basis of existing tenancies. Moreover the names Baxter, Carwood
and Wilkie can be followed through the 17th century as owners
and tenants succeeded one another. In 1653 for example John
Baxter's grandson, a cordiner and citizen of London, took
possession of the first floor house. Lady Johnson's 'principal
dwelling house' passed from Margaret Carwood and her husband
James Macgill in 1623 to James Kinnoche of Blairquone, but the
couple kept their booths and nether cellar until 1628, selling them
to David Wemyss. In 1655 Thomas Spens the Baker enjoyed the
rent of three houses in Mossman's tenement and this consolidation
of a holding may have been the cue for the rationalisation of the
property by levels. In the same year a lawyer took possession of
Captain Davidson's house from his heirs Janet and Sara Davidson,
along with the stone shop which was still linked to the 'last
dwelling house'.[3]
As for the Mossmans they retained their share of the building
until the middle of the 17th century. In 1635 Richard Mossman, a
younger son of John and grandson of James, passed the ground
floor house and booth, once occupied by Murdoch Brown, along
with other family property to his sister Mariota, probably in
preparation for his emigration. In 1657 Mariota's husband John
Hamilton, a Reader in the Protestant Kirk, was still registered as
the owner of this property but the Mossmans were looking to new
opportunities in the American colonies, some by way of the Ulster
Plantations. Their name fades from the records though the House
in the Netherbow continued to be referred to as the tenement of
the late James Mossman even as late as 1764.[4]
Many gaps remain to be filled in the overall picture but there is
little evidence of structural change during this period apart from
the new doorways to which I have referred and the steady addition
of new buildings to the rear, closing the space between the
backland and the next tenement. What must have changed
dramatically however were the furnishings and decorations.
In James Mossman's time there would have been very few items

of furniture outwith benches, tables and kists, though prosperous households may have owned a principal bed and some carved chairs.[5] The elaborate panelling, some of which dates to the 16th century, certainly puts the Netherbow house in this league. Throughout the 17th century the Scots followed the Dutch in adding dressers, elaborate chairs and settles, tiles, hangings and pictures. Depending on the affluence and social position of the occupier each part of the House in the Netherbow must have gained progressively more furniture.

One outstanding feature of the house however remains a puzzle – the painted ceiling on the second floor. The work of local craftsmen drawing on pattern books, the ceiling is a rumbustious, crude and vigorous offshoot of the much more orderly and 'finished' ceilings known to us at Prestonpans, Crathie and elsewhere. The ceiling breathes, not to say gusts, the atmosphere of a late Renaissance baroque energy, replete, despite the Reformation, with emblem, fable and an earthy sense of the magical. It apes the taste of the magnates and great lairds without their resources of patronage. Unless Lady Johnson was a particularly merry widow it seems unlikely that she commissioned this work especially as she was only a tenant. The possiblility of a Mossman connection cannot entirely be ruled out since some of the earliest painted timbers such as those at Kinneil are mid-16th century and Mossman's tastes did follow the Court at one remove. The date however seems very early and the style a little beneath the Mossman level. Perhaps James Kinnoche of Blairquone, who bought the principal dwelling house in 1628, entertained his friends under an exuberant newly painted ceiling. Later as the fashion of open timber waned, the ceiling was decorously boarded over and preserved to the present day in its original though much faded colours.[6]

By the late 18th century the Old Town of Edinburgh was in decline. Conditions had become intolerably overcrowded and insanitary, and the old stairhead democracy was breaking down in the quest for more cultivated manners and language. David Allan's view of the High Street, dated 1793, tells the whole story in a detailed portrayal of the House in the Netherbow. The ground floor shops are still in business including a bookseller and, under the outside stairs, a maker of 'legs, arms and artificial limbs and snuff boxes'. Above, the first floor is now a saddler's, the second a servants' agency, while in the attic a poor scholar offers tuition in Hebrew, Greek and Latin, in company with a dealer in 'side meal and barley'.[7]

Further decline and the transfer of the respectable classes to the New Town of Edinburgh were to heap worse indignities on the House in the Netherbow before very different social and religious developments came to its rescue.

NOTES

1. Jim Gilhooley's account of the history of Cant's Tenement is held by the Edinburgh Old Town Renewal Trust, whose office was originally located in that building.
2. *Protocol Book of Alexander Guthrie*, 22 May 1600.
3. These references are culled from manuscript sources in the Edinburgh City Archives including the Inventories of the Moses Bundles and Abstracts of the protocol books.
4. Moses Bundles 7 J.W. 21/10/1764.
5. See I. Gow *The Scottish Interior* (Edinburgh, 1993).
6. See M.R. Apted *The Painted Ceilings of Scotland 1550–1650*, (Edinburgh, 1966).
7. *Edinburgh, High Street*, engraving by David Allan in the National Gallery of Scotland.

CHAPTER SEVEN

JOHN KNOX'S HOUSE

It is hard to ascertain when the House in the Netherbow began to be described as 'John Knox's House'. In her *Guide to the Beauties of Scotland*, the Honourable Mrs Murray mentions the 'tottering bow window to a house; whence Knox thundered his addresses to the people', a clear reference to the picturesque timber window which had been built over James Mossman's Renaissance ornament and which is prominent in many early 19th century prints. Mrs Murray's Guide was published in 1799 but is based on a visit in 1784. Her observation can be confirmed from the detailed topographical study of the High Street by David Allan which is dated 1793 and shows the sculptured figure on the corner of the house as the Reformer along with 'Knox the Bookseller's' on the ground floor. When Stark's 'Picture of Edinburgh' was published in 1806 the House in the Netherbow is confidently described as 'the House of the great Scottish Reformer John Knox', and every guide book thereafter followed this line.

The origins of the ascription to Knox are even harder to gauge.

There may have been an oral tradition connecting Knox to the House in the Netherbow. Against this is the fact that even in 1764 the notaries – that most conservative of breeds – were still referring to the property as Mossman's Tenement, though this is the last such reference that I have been able to trace.[1]

It seems more likely that the link between Knox and the house was established at a time when the oral traditions about the burgh and its inhabitants were breaking down and being lost, just as the Old Town itself was losing the broad social structure which had characterised it in previous centuries. There was also the confusion of nearby Trunk's Close (once known as Knox's Close) where, according to different versions, another John Knox had once resided, or where one of Knox's several Manses (formerly the town house of the Abbot of Dunfermline) had been situated.[2]

In addition the House in the Netherbow was manifestly something different and special; what could be more appropriate than that here the 'Apostle of the Scots' had lived. The identification of Knox's house is also part of the Romantic rediscovery of Scottish history, and of Knox's role in this rediscovery as a hero displaying the characteristically Scottish virtues of independence, moral earnestness and piety. The fact that the house was very old and the sculptured figure on the facade barely recognisable only added to the emotional reverence with which the building rapidly came to be associated.

In 1811 Thomas McCrie's epoch-making *Life of John Knox* explicitly tied the account of Knox's last days with the Netherbow house. This supplied another part of the growing legend as Smeton's description of Knox's final sermon (first published in 1579) was translated into images of Knox being helped by weeping attendants down the High Street to the Netherbow.

> After he had blessed the people with his wonted cheerful spirit, but with feeble body, and leaning on his staff, he departed to his house accompanied by almost the whole meeting, from which he did not afterwards come out alive.[3]

Sometime after 1814 when St George's Church was built the ambiguous stone figure was provided with an oak canopy and pulpit, modelled on the pulpit of the new church.

Finally in 1824, in the first edition of his classic *Traditions of Edinburgh*, Robert Chambers achieves the full apotheosis in his account of John Knox's House.

> Close beneath the window there has long existed a curious effigy of the Reformer stuck upon the corner and apparently holding forth to the passers-by. Of this no features were for a long time discernible till Mr Drymen (then tenant of the house) took shame to himself for the neglect it was experiencing and got it daubed over in glaring oil colours at his own expense. Thus a red nose and two intensely black eyes were brought strongly out on the mass of the face and a pair of white iron Geneva bands completed the resuscitation.[4]

This description is omitted in later editions of the Traditions but the fully articulated legend indicating Knox's study, the window from which he preached, and even a small room which served as a baptistery is retained as orthodoxy. When he came to Edinburgh the stonemason and geologist Hugh Miller was typical in paying his respects at this by now hallowed site of Protestant pilgrimage.

John Knox House *c.* 1840, following the collapse of Lord Balmerino's House in 1839. Drawing and lithograph by L. Ghémar.

John Knox House and Moubray House in 1843 following the collapse of Lord Balmerino's House to the east in 1839 and the demolition of the High Street houses to the west as part of the major scheme for 'Improvement', which also created whole new streets such as Cockburn and Victoria Street.

Early photographic image or calotype of John Knox House c. 1845. This is an early print held in the John Knox House Museum. Calotypes of three images of John Knox House, including this one, are held in the Hill Adamson Archive in the collection of the Scottish National Portrait Gallery. This image clearly shows the semi-ruinous condition of the building which led to legal moves for its demolition.

The newly-formed Free Church of Scotland spearheaded the campaign to save John Knox House. The initial plans of the appeal committee for the site were nothing, if not ambitious, as this sketch shows. The aim was a worthy monument to Scotland's national hero and to its new national Church. Realism set in as the Free Church struggled to build a new church in every Scottish parish.

John Knox House in 1900 showing the exterior Hippolyte Blanc's repair and restoration work in 1886. Note the completed Knox's Free Church next door, which was opened in 1853.

John Knox House *c.* 1920, after William Hay became Curator of the John Knox House Museum and opened his well-known bookshop on the ground floor.

The John Knox House Museum opened to the public in 1853. This stained-glass portrait of John Knox was made and gifted to the museum by James Ballantine in 1863.

This unattributed print is a fine example of the romanticised views of John Knox House which took hold in the late 19th century.

The social history of John Knox House offers a different picture. This section of windowless cellar was used as a dwelling-house well into the 19th century. Photograph by Anne Maxwell.

William J. Hay's *Old Houses in Edinburgh* (undated) with drawings by Bruce Home was an ambitious attempt to awaken interest in what was left of the medieval Old Town. Most of the drawings date to between 1880 and 1910 and provide a unique record of the Old Town in decay, though the book also includes romanticised 'reconstructions'. This drawing shows the back of John Knox House and the extensions built over Lord Hope's Court which have now been demolished.

The survey of restoration work of 1990 exposed these booths on the south side of John Knox House. Originally open to the street, each section would contain a separate shop or stall, and customers would come in under the timbered gallery to inspect their wares. Photograph by Anne Maxwell.

This cultural formation of 'John Knox's House', irrespective of the historical case for and against the Knox connection, is in itself a fascinating topic. But the Knox link was soon to become crucial to the survival of the House in any form.

From 1791 the Dean of Guild Court records reflect the decay of the House in the Netherbow. In that year the upper storeys had fallen into disrepair and legal action was taken by one proprietor to make the roof watertight. In 1798 another action was brought to recover a share of the cost of roof repairs from a negligent owner. The house figures frequently in the Court processes from then on until, on 17 February 1839, the adjoining tenement, known as Lord Balmerino's House, collapsed and the remains had to be demolished. On 18 February the Dean of Guild officer reported that another house 'commonly called John Knox's Land' was 'in an insufficient and dangerous state to the inhabitants thereof and the public' due to the collapse. In 1847 a petition to the magistrates asserted that the fourth storey of 'Knox's Land' had 'lain waste and uninhabited for three years' and sought permission to demolish.[5]

This picture of serious decline and decay can be confirmed from the 18th and 19th century titles held by The Church of Scotland, the house's present owners. They reflect a position of fragmented ownership in which merchants, lawyers and minor gentry have been replaced by painters, pewterers and spirit dealers, and even a baker whose first floor oven threatened to burn down the whole premises. An interesting undated note on these deeds mentions that the cellars had all been converted into dwelling houses. Such was the fate of an overcrowded and poverty ridden Old Town after the withdrawal of the respectable classes to more salubrious quarters in the New Town.

A third unique source gives a vivid and concrete picture of 'Knox's Land'. This is the model prepared in 1850 by the architect James Johnstone of the house, with the existing shops and booths on the ground floor. These include an umbrella maker's, a painter's shop and a dram shop or spirit dealer.[6]

Remarkably despite the fall in social tone, and the enclosure of the 'forebooth' on the south side by a screening wall, the shape and division of the shops is exactly the same as that laid out in the transactions of 22 May 1600. The accuracy of the 1850 model was vouchsafed in 1990 by the discovery of a partially obscured painted shop sign on the newly exposed west frontage. What the model does not reveal is the critical state of repair of the house leading into the carefully planned repairs of this period. However a surviving photograph from the 1840s confirms the pitiful condition of the roof and the deserted and all but ruinous upper storeys.

Salvation however was already to hand in the shape of an alliance between the Society of Antiquaries of Scotland and the newly formed Free Church of Scotland which took the lead in raising Protestant tempers against the sacrilege of demolition. Court action was taken to stay the sentence of execution, public meetings were held, subscriptions raised, and notable citizens including Lord Cockburn, James Bannatyne the popular writer and artist, David Roberts the painter and many more, lent their names and in some cases their pockets to the cause of restoration.

The effort to save John Knox's House is perhaps the first instance of a conservation campaign in Scottish life, though most of the participants were not primarily motivated by the building as much as by its associations. Fortunately, given that background, the house was well served by those put in charge of the successive phases of its repair and restoration, notably James Smith (the Royal Master Mason of his day), James Johnstone, and Hippolyte Blanc.

Mossman or Roytell's ornamental window on the west facade was uncovered, the roofs and upper galleries repaired, and the external sculpture 'restored' by Handyside Ritchie, probably with reference to continental parallels. In 1849 the stonework of the west facade was carefully numbered, taken down and rebuilt. One room was lost at the rear of the building on the first floor and a new gable consolidated with metal rods. The eastern gable was also secured despite the loss of Balmerino's Land. There is little reference in notes about these repairs to internal features though in 1863 James Ballantyne's stained glass portrait of Knox was gifted and installed on the second floor.[7]

The documentation for Hippolyte Blanc's restoration of 1886 is even fuller and includes the tradesmens' invoices carefully checked and authorised along with Blanc's own report. The main works were again structural with the rear wall the source of trouble since the east gable was now supported by the Knox Church which the Free Church had built between 1850 and 1853 to complement their ownership of John Knox's House.

Blanc's work however went further with regard to the interior of the house and involved the 'perfecting of wall panelling in the chief apartment where damaged'. This has been cited against Blanc but unjustly since he is quite explicit about the existing panelling.

> Though of slightly mixed character in detail the wall panelling has every experience of being genuine, and fortunately is in perfect preservation.

Blanc's expressed aim was

> to complete neglected portions, bring the apartments into harmony with themselves and with the period they represent and so increase the public interest so widely evoked of late years.

Some of the features introduced by Blanc such as new panelling in the rear rooms have since been removed but most of his good work has stood the test of time. It was also Blanc who articulated the excellent principle that 'national antiquities only of the 16th century should be collected', though this guidance was not unfortunately followed.

The House in the Netherbow first opened as a museum in 1853 and was one of the earliest examples of a privately owned public museum in Scotland. It continued under the ownership of the Free Church of Scotland and the United Free Church of Scotland until the union with the Auld Kirk in 1929 brought The Church of Scotland into being. The emphasis throughout was on the role of the house as a memorial to the Reformer and a significant collection of pictures, books and other memorabilia was soon gathered reflecting not only Knox's achievements but their continuation in the Covenanting period and through the Fathers of the Free Church such as Thomas Chalmers. Although the Society of Antiquaries had been instrumental in the initial campaign and rescue it was Free Church money and persistence that had bought up the various parts of the house and the adjoining site of Balmerino's collapsed tenement. Contemporary plans for a monumental church building on the vacant site, though succeeded more realistically and modestly by the Knox Church, reveal just how highly the expanding denomination rated the symbolic importance of the site as a potential counterweight to the Established Kirk's continuing possession of St Giles. The Knox

Church, now named Moray-Knox, was demolished in 1970 to make way for The Netherbow Arts Centre.

The Disruption background also illuminates or in this case darkens the controversy about the authenticity of the house's link with Knox, which blew up in the 1880s following Blanc's restoration, and continued to attract interest into the 1890s. The disproportionate heat generated by this apparently academic argument derives from the social and religious divisions which the Disruption had crystallised across Scotland, replicating in every community the key institutions of religion and education.

On one side of the argument was the Free Church interest represented by their legal adviser Lord Guthrie who produced an excellent handbook to John Knox House, the historical value of which remains despite his sometimes tortuous lines of reasoning when it came to the issue of Knox's residence.[8] On the other side was Robert Miller, an Edinburgh Baillie and 'auld kirker', whose thorough researches were designed to vindicate the Dean of Guild's Court and the Town Council, and expose what he saw as the Free Church 'sanctification' of the house. Miller's closely argued book 'John Knox and the Town Council' is often sarcastic in tone and refers provocatively to 'the Secession known as the Free Church'. Caught between these redoubtable contestants were the Antiquaries who were anxious to maintain historical accuracy but also reluctant to detract from the importance of the house and their satisfaction at its preservation.[9]

The articles and books generated by the John Knox House controversy contain the first serious modern research on the House in the Netherbow but tended to focus attention away from the building itself. As in previous centuries the fortunes of this remarkable building were placed in a much wider social and cultural arena, and the question of whether John Knox ever lived there generated as much heat as light.

NOTES

1. Since there is no comprehensive index to Edinburgh Sasines later references may exist.
2. See P. Miller 'John Knox and his Manse' in *Proceedings of the Society of Antiquaries of Scotland*, vol. XXV (Edinburgh, 1891) and R. Miller *John Knox and the Town Council of Edinburgh* (Edinburgh, 1898).
3. See D. Laing (ed.), *The Works of John Knox* (Edinburgh, 1864), vol. vi,

pp. 634–44 and 654–60 for Thomas Smeton's account of Knox's last illness and death.

4. R. Chambers, *Traditions of Edinburgh* (Edinburgh, 1824), vol.1, pp. 245–46.

5. These references draw on Robert Miller's account in *John Knox and the Town Council of Edinburgh* (Edinburgh, 1898). Miller was himself a Dean of Guild and his arguments are based on a thorough examination of the Court records.

6. The model is on display in the John Knox House Museum.

7. These restorations are well documented in the Edinburgh Room of the City's Central Library, which holds *John Knox's House*, an undated (c. 1851) manuscript account by James Johnstone, and a manuscript report by Hippolyte Blanc on *John Knox's House* dated 8 February 1886, which also includes information on the 1853 work, Blanc's drawings and the tradesmens' accounts.

8. See C.J. Guthrie 'Is "John Knox's House" Entitled to the Name?' in *Proceedings of the Society of Antiquaries of Scotland*, vol. XXV (Edinburgh, 1891) and 'The Traditional Belief in John Knox's House at the Netherbow vindicated', *Ibid.* vol. XXXIII (Edinburgh, 1899).

9. See Sir D. Wilson, 'Supplementary Notes on John Knox's House, Netherbow, Edinburgh' in *Proceedings of the Society of Antiquaries of Scotland*, (Edinburgh, 1891) and P. Miller, 'Supplementary Notes on John Knox's House', *Ibid* vol. XXVII (Edinburgh, 1893).

CHAPTER EIGHT

HISTORY AND CULTURE

Victorian debate on the authenticity of 'John Knox's' House had no impact on the popularity of the museum or its secure place as one of the attractions of Old Edinburgh. The appeal of history combined with the new phenomenon of leisure for both the middle and working classes, anticipated the 20th century destiny of the High Street as a tourist location, even if some of the tourists came from no farther afield than Musselburgh or Dunfermline. The irony is that the late-Victorian cult of Scottish heritage overlapped with drastic 'improvements' in the Old Town which swept away many of the older buildings and even whole streets, leaving the House in the Netherbow and its neighbour Moubray House, isolated survivals from the medieval burgh.

The part played by John Knox House in these cultural developments was based on both its historic and its religious importance, underpinned by Hippolyte Blanc's 1886 restoration which was gauged to satisfy contemporary taste. The real flowering of John Knox House as a visitor centre however was the achievement of its longest serving curator, William Hay.

Hay set up his 'Old Edinburgh Arts and Crafts' business in the ground floors of John Knox House and Moubray House in 1911, connecting the two premises with a gallery at the rear. This was no souvenir shop but an enterprising artistic venture based on a discerning appreciation of Scottish crafts – the Royal Mile's first craft centre. Behind Hay's enthusiasm were Ruskin, William Morris and their Scottish associates such as James Ballantine whose stained glass workshops in Carrubbers Close had revived the medieval art in Scotland and created an international centre of excellence. The windows and shop gate, which still characterize the Moubray House shop, clearly exhibit the 'arts and crafts' influence which Patrick Geddes, among others, was fostering so vigorously in Edinburgh. Unfortunately, as with so many succeeding craft centres of quality, Edinburgh's public showed itself unwilling to back Hay's artistic tastes and the venture was wound up due to the economic pressures of the First World War.

Hay however continued the responsibility he had undertaken for the John Knox House Museum in 1911. He gave up the Moubray House shop and developed a bookselling and publishing operation on the ground floor of the Netherbow house. The combination of museum and bookshop proved successful and survived until 1957 when Mr Hay's son Carmen Hay retired, only a few years after his father's death.

The role of the Curator of the John Knox House Museum was controlled by William Hay's agreement with his Church landlords. The existing exhibits and the overall structure of the museum remained in its late-Victorian form with the rooms named in line with Chamber's 'Traditions', and well-stocked with books in glass cases, prints and furniture. Hay was careful however not to describe the house as John Knox's Manse, espousing the minimal version of the connection with Knox, ie. that the Reformer had died in the house during the siege of Edinburgh Castle.

Hay's enterprise and creativity found outlet through the shop and his publishing activities. He produced an excellent series of Old Edinburgh postcards, a penny guide to the Royal Mile from Edinburgh Castle to the Palace of Holyroodhouse, and a few outstanding books on the history of the Old Town. These include an excellent history of the Guild of Hammermen by John Smith which contains important material on the Chapel of St Eloi in St Giles and a remarkable record of the Old Town in change and decay, *Houses in Old Edinburgh*, which is mainly the work of the artist Bruce J. Home undertaken with Hay's encouragement. These volumes along with the woodcut commissioned by Hay as a logo for the House, and even the handsome tickets of admission, display his sense of culture and commitment to quality. Not surprisingly the books did not have mass appeal and they were the cause of some financial setbacks, so restricting their publisher's output.

William Hay's legacy was his success in interweaving history, culture and tourism together as a unified expression of his knowledge and enthusiasm. In time Hay became an Old Town character in his own right and so part of the story which he was engaged in relating. The bookshop has its place in contemporary memories alongside the renowned pawnshop which Esther Henry set up in the Moubray House premises which Hay had earlier vacated. The Curator of John Knox House and the Jewish pawnbroker continued to make use of the connecting gallery at the rear to 'mind each other's shops' during quiet spells!

The gap left by the retiral of the Hay family from their 56 year occupancy of the Curator's post was filled by Harry Linley of Kinloch Anderson, the well known Edinburgh kiltmakers. For over 30 years until his retiral in 1989, Linley combined his enthusiasm for Scottish history and experise in tartans with shrewd management of the kilt shop which was installed in the ground floor of John Knox House. Harry Linley's great contribution to the museum lay in the devoted care which he took of the building ensuring in cooperation with his landlords a substantial programme of maintenance and repairs, as well as the uncovering and conservation of the painted ceiling.

The new Curator also instituted changes in the museum contents sweeping away some of the clutter of presbyterian memorabilia, though without finding a fully satisfactory way of presenting the history of the house and the story of John Knox in combination. The link with Kinloch Anderson through Harry Linley provided stability and security for the House in the Netherbow through some severe fluctuations in the fortunes of the High Street. In the 1950s many people were moved out to peripheral housing schemes, leaving the Victorian and Edwardian 'Old Town' depopulated, dilapidated and in some parts abandoned. A beleaguered tourism sector came to depend on Scottish staples such as Tartan.

Harry Linley's retiral in 1989 coincided with another change of era in Edinburgh's Old Town as a concerted effort to renovate the historic fabric and bring people back to the area began to bear fruit. In 1972 The Church of Scotland had completed a new building on the site of the Moray-Knox Church, The Netherbow Arts Centre. This was a successor to the Kirk's Gateway Theatre on Leith Walk which had been sold to Scottish Television after the establishment of the Edinburgh Civic Theatre at the Royal Lyceum. The aim of both Gateway and Netherbow was to provide a meeting place, and a centre of cross fertilisation, between two streams of modern Scottish life, religion and culture. Since the mid-1980s The Netherbow had been closely involved in efforts to renew the community life of the Old Town for the benefit of both residents and visitors, and it was to The Netherbow that the

Church of Scotland turned to take John Knox House forward in this changed climate.

In response to the challenge The Netherbow undertook a thorough examination and survey of the House in the Netherbow under the supervision of Benjamin Tindall Architects. The late medieval fabric was carefully exposed, particularly on the ground floor where later shop fittings had obscured the original pattern internally and externally. The stone booths revealed by this exercise are the only surviving medieval shops in Scotland and a tribute to the goldsmith's taste and money which disdained the normal wooden 'luckenbooths'. The discovery of the Renaissance book fragments and the preservation, beneath William Hay's Edwardian shop front, of Mossman's frontage, were a bonus.

Following the detailed physical survey and conservation work, a new exhibition was installed in the museum, combining fidelity to the the purpose of the founders in creating a memorial to John Knox, with a full account of the building's history and the Mossman inheritance. This proved easier than might have been expected since taken together Knox and Mossman provide a full and complementary picture of the religious and cultural life of 16th century Scotland. The cultural theme was taken up with a new direct link between John Knox House and the Arts Centre, also giving access to the visitor facilities of cafe and toilets. This finally improved on the Victorian addition of one toilet and waste pipe to the previously pipeless medieval mansion!

Throughout this process William Hay was a guiding influence. His logo was reintroduced in a slightly amended form to represent this fresh marriage of old and new, religion and culture. The task the newly combined centre set itself was to develop a relationship appropriate to the late 20th century and to the decades ahead. The House in the Netherbow is a place of importance for residents, visitors and overseas tourists alike. It is a superior and unique cultural artefact imbued with historic, cultural and religious importance. It is also a building in which people can move, explore and create – a place of learning in both the old and the modern senses of that word.

It is much harder from within this process to discern the key trends of our period of the house's history, and of the life of Edinburgh. From Hie Gait to High Street, then to Royal Mile, and now Old Town, the area around the Netherbow has seen many changes since people first established the burgh as a focus of communal life. No doubt it will see many more. But whatever social, economic and cultural changes lie ahead, we must not be seduced by the cash registers of the 'heritage industry' into forgetting that the only lasting and truly interesting foundation of civic life is the personality and achievement of our people, past, present and future. On that at least, even James Mossman and John Knox could agree.

JOHN KNOX HOUSE

Plans and Sketches

John Knox House, 1990. Sketch by Iain Stewart, of Benjamin Tindall Architects.

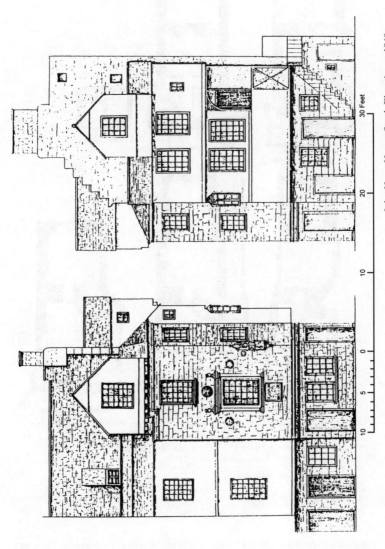

John Knox House, West Elevation, *c.* 1860. Drawing by W. J. McCulloch, Architect.

John Knox House, South Elevation, *c.* 1860.
Drawing by W. J. McCulloch, Architect.

30 Feet

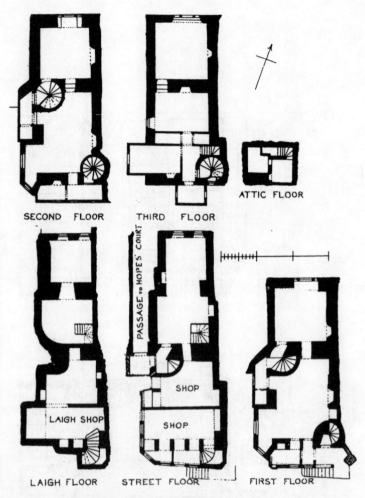

SECOND FLOOR

THIRD FLOOR

ATTIC FLOOR

PASSAGE ᴛᴏ HOPE'S COURT

LAIGH SHOP

SHOP

SHOP

LAIGH FLOOR

STREET FLOOR

FIRST FLOOR

Ground plan of John Knox House *c.* 1890 from MacGibbon and Ross
The Castellated and Domestic Architecture of Scotland (1892).

Please see opposite page (p.57):

The ground plans of John Knox House *c.* 1890 annotated with the occupiers of Mossman's
Land in 1600. The continuity of the subdivisions on the ground and basement levels
through to the Victorian era is remarkable, and was borne out both by the architect's model
of *c.* 1850 which is still displayed in the John Knox House Museum and the survey of
1990–91.

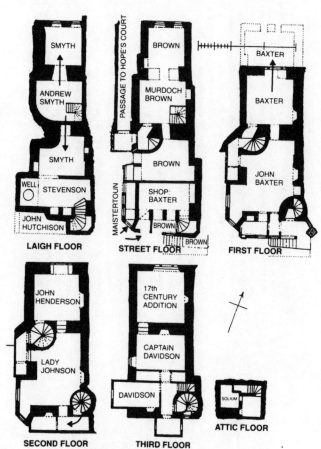

MOSSMAN'S LAND IN 1600

Laigh Floor:	Access from Lord Hope's Close. 3 cellars a. Andrew Smyth, spurrier/cutler b. Well? or pit c. Cellar below Baxter's booth - Widow Stevenson d. Nether cellar, below easter forebooth
Street Floor:	a. Murdoch Brown's house - hall & 2 chambers b. Stane shop or booth - West side: Maistertoun, merchant c. Baxter's shop - tailor d. Easter forebooth - Murdoch Brown, bonnetmaker e. The 'penteis' - Murdoch Brown, bonnetmaker
First Floor:	Baxter's house - hall & 2 chambers, one within the other
Second Floor:	a. Back house b. Principal dwelling at the head of the turnpike - one hall & 2 forestairs
Third Floor & Attic:	a. 17th-century addition b. Captain Davidson's last dwelling house - hall, chamber, & 'seat' above the turnpike

57

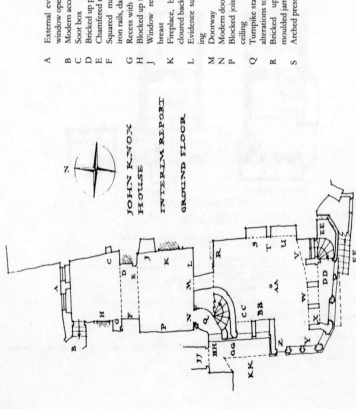

JOHN KNOX HOUSE

INTERIM REPORT

GROUND FLOOR

A External evidence of alterations to window openings
B Modern access to Moubray House
C Soot box
D Bricked up press with giblet checks
E Chamfered rybats
F Squared masonry pier supporting iron rails, dated 1874
G Recess with isolated chamfered rybat
H Blocked up fireplace
J Window recess with blocked up breast
K Fireplace, blocked up and breast cloured back
L Evidence suggesting window opening
M Doorway
N Modern doorway in brick
P Blocked joist sockets below existing ceiling
Q Turnpike stair – evidence suggesting alterations to treads
R Bricked up fireplace with roll moulded jamb
S Arched press

T Cloured face of pier suggesting line partition
U Arched press with timber member in wall
V Squinch supporting turnpike stair
W Piers with chamfered rybats, iron crooks, stone lintels
X Continuous masonry construction
Y Moulded window openings
Z Moulded door openings
AA Cast iron column
BB Piers with chamfered rybats and evidence of sill
CC Door opening
DD Brickwork wall with door and windows
EE Stair to basement
FF Forestair
GG Window to Turnpike stair
HH Door to turnpike stair
FF Painted timber lintel
JJ Head of Hope's Close
KK Projecting timber structure continuous with internal joists. Corbel in NE corner

Ground floor plan of John Knox House annotated from the survey of 1990 carried out by Benjamin Tindall Architects.

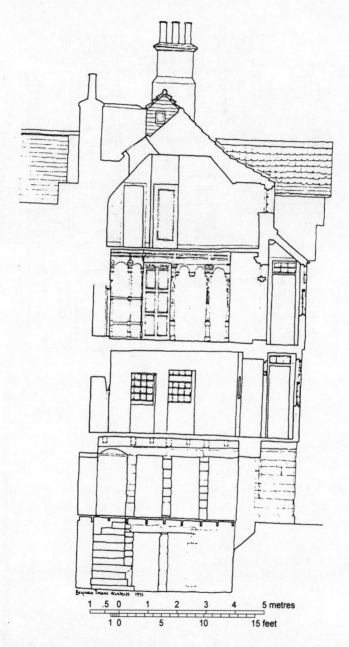

1 .5 0   1   2   3   4   5 metres

1 0   5   10   15 feet

John Knox House East-West section based on survey of 1990–91 by Benjamin Tindall Architects.

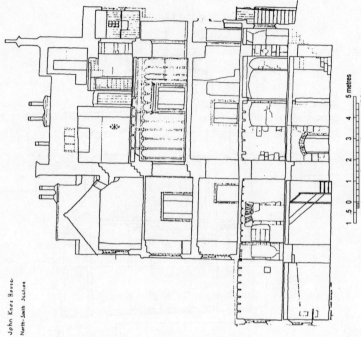

John Knox House
North-South Section

John Knox House, North-South section, based on survey of 1990–91 by Benjamin Tindall Architects.

JOHN KNOX HOUSE
A BRIEF TOUR

Exterior

1 Look up the broad High Street designed as a market street. The original street-line continues through the thick dividing wall inside John Knox House.
2 The Netherbow section of the High Street provided a protective narrowing for the city gate, first at the top then at the foot of the 'bow'.
3 The house at the head of the bow: look out for
   (a) the projecting timber galleries – exposed on the west side
   (b) the entrances to the foreland and the backland
   (c) the ashlar stone frontage with Doric columns
   (d) the Mossman coat of arms ('love lintel')
   (e) the 'Moses' sundial
   (f) the New Testament motto which reads, in English, 'Love God above all and your neighbour as yourself'.

Interior: the Booths and Shops

On the ground floor spot

   (a) The enclosed arcade on the south side. Walk in between the pillars and look back to the original 'outside' wall.
   (b) The 'stane buiths'. These booths are the only surviving medieval 'shops' in Scotland.
   (c) The beams on which fragments of sixteenth century books were found in 1990.
   (d) The massive wall between foreland and backland: evidence of an earlier house at the head of the Netherbow with 'semi-fortified' walls – compare slender pillars in Mossman's house.
   (e) The Museum introduction in the backland with 'Knox's Pulpit' and a model of the house in 1840 before the first Victorian restoration: note the shops.
   (f) The turnpike stair with its door and 'ingle light' for looking out to see who was there.

(g) Stair levels have been altered in line with the raising of the backland floor to be more level with the front.

First floor: back

(a) Look at back window to see remains of 'collapsed room' which formed the rear room of the backland – note the blackened chimney stones and the weathered moulding of the fireplace.

(b) Some of the books illustrate the work of early Edinburgh printers (James Bassandyne and Robert Lapraik) whose workshops were in the Netherbow.

(c) Note first English Bible to be printed in Scotland (Bassandyne's Bible) and Knox's portraits and books.

(d) Look at 19th century picture of Knox by William Dyce – related to unfinished picture by David Wilkie in the National Gallery.

First floor: front

(a) Go to the front gallery room and look up to the castle where James Mossman served under Sir William Kirkcaldy of Grange.

(b) See the coins and medallions and the reconstructed goldsmith's workbench. The ceramic wall plaques show the royal succession during the time that the Mossmans were officers of the Royal Mint.

(c) St Eloi or Eligius, Patron Saint of the Goldsmiths, is placed in an original niche. The statue is based on a surviving medieval statue, probably from Glasgow Cathedral.

(d) Scottish Renaissance court music plays in the background.

(e) Finish back in west gallery with the different entrances showing the original divisions into foreland and backland. The direct passages between front and back show a later more logical division of the house by floors.

Second floor: back

(a) The Dutch tiles may not be original to this house but saved from another 'land' during the Victorian 'improvements'.

(b) The 'Sermon' of John Knox is drawn from The Scots Confession of 1560. The psalm singing from the contemporary Church of Scotland General Assembly.

(c) The portrait medallion of Knox in stained glass is from the workshop of James Ballantine and gifted by him to the house in 1850's. Note the wrong birth date. Knox was born in 1513.

(d) The framed painting of Lot and his daughters may come originally from a painted ceiling in the Dean Mansion.

(e) Note difference in levels between front and back rooms.

Second floor: front

(a) Though altered and perhaps 'improved' the panelling is original – 16th century with 17th century additions. Note the 1561 date in the gallery room – the year of Mary's return from France.

(b) See the door knocker ('dead as a door nail') on west door.

(c) Note inlay on door to gallery room.

(d) The 'wall painting' of Cain and Abel was saved from the ceiling of the Dean Mansion – early 17th century. See the 19th century addition near west window – popularly believed to have been painted by a lodger in lieu of rent!

(e) Note original oak timbers on floor.

(f) Tape of Knox and Mary is based on Knox's own account in his History of the Reformation as expanded by playwright James Bridie.

(g) Painted ceiling early 17th century – a crude and rumbustious variation on this notable feature of Scottish 16th and 17th century interior decoration. Figures and patterns taken from 'pattern books' by local painters representing classical motifs and 'grotesquerie' and 'diablerie' of the late Renaissance/early Baroque. Though much faded, the colours are *original*. The ceiling was later covered up as tastes changed and therefore preserved.

(h) Reproduction kist based on a Jacobean vestment chest long associated with the house but lost in the 1950's. Carved and moulded by George Blackhall.

Attic and loft (not open to the public)

A complete dwelling house to which an additional room has been added. Note the massive corbels indicating the gable of The Netherbow house probably connected with the building of the King's Wall after 1470.

Loft room fitted out as 19th century slum dwelling.

JOHN KNOX HOUSE
CHRONOLOGY AND DEVELOPMENT

1 The wooden house on the market street is replaced by a stone-built two-storey house, something of which survives in the backland of the present John Knox House – any time from 1450. Note the later loss of the back chamber of this house on the second floor.

2 Alexander Boncle builds a new 'Netherbow' to narrow the approach to the Port and assigns the house at the head of the bow to his son-in-law Walter Reidpath, goldsmith (1472). The north gable wall of this house still survives with its massive corbels, indicating a three-storey house of very solid construction.

3 The Netherbow Port is moved (1513–1517) after the Battle of Flodden.

4 Christina Reidpath marries John Arres (c.1500). Then or later the house at the head of the bow passes to Christina and in 1525 to Christina's son, John Arres, while Christina and her husband retain the liferent. During this period, or perhaps after 5. below, it is likely that the house was reconstructed and improved, perhaps in association with the house on the site of the present arts centre (later known as Lord Balmerino's house) which was also owned by the Reidpath family.

5 The 'Rough Wooing' of the Earl of Hertford – 1544. The Netherbow Port is blown up – some damage to the house likely.

6 On 10th January 1555 the house passes into the ownership of Mariota Arres (daughter of John and granddaughter of Christina) following the death of her father. With the approval of her guardians (Alexander Mossman and Sir George Littlejohn) the house is leased to John Mossman, goldsmith and his second wife Isobel Dee.

7 On 27th July 1556 James Mossman as heir apparent of John receives land in Forrester's Wynd the life-rent being reserved to John and Isobel Dee. This sasine refers to Mariota Arres, *his affianced wife*, while a further transaction on the same day assigns John Knox House to the joint ownership of James Mossman

and Mariota Arres. These transactions all form part of a *nuptial contract*. In 1558 John Mossman dies.

8 Post 1556 James and Mariota embark on a major reconstruction and enhancement of the house which gives it substantially its present shape. Southern and western galleries and facades, the booths, the attics and possibly the cellars all owe their current layout and in the main appearance to this reconstruction. The adjustment to the treads on the west stair may belong to this period as may the raising of the ceiling on the ground floor of the backland. The following important points are made by Peter Miller

> 'In none of the sasines affecting this tenement at the Netherbow is there any reference made to its occupants, the presumption being, from the unique character of the building, its elaborate ornamentation, and having the arms of the owner emblazoned upon it, with the initials of James Mosman and Mariot Arres his spouse also displayed upon it, along with the special legal formalities taken before the marriage, and the subsequent legal proceedings taken in 1568 and 1571 were made to ensure unbroken possession and occupation of the house as the family mansion. None of the other properties belonging to Mariot Arres are disposed of and protected in any of the sasines in this special manner.' (*Proceedings of the Society of Antiquities*, 9 February 1981, p.152).

9 In 1572 Sir James Mossman is outlawed and his property made forfeit. In 1573 he is executed. After his death his widow (Janet King, his second wife) may have been able to recover the Netherbow house immediately on the basis of a marriage settlement. At any rate the family was gradually able to buy back its property.

10 Janet King further sub-divides and lets the property. The sasines of 1600 when she relinquishes ownership indicate a number of shops and residential tenants, as well as five separate cellars.

11 In the seventeenth century the property was reordered to provide more houses by levels, including the foreland rooms and backland rooms. An extra floor was added to the backland. In 1647 three houses in John Knox House (probably on three levels) were owned by a master baker Thomas Spens. The same process occurred in the land in Advocate's Close post 1600 as a deliberate development for leasing purposes. The connecting

door on the second floor is probably 17th century. The enclosure of the ground floor galleries around the booths or shops is probably also a 17th century development.

12 The model of the house which was made before the first victorian restoration (c.1850) shows the house as it appeared in the 18th and early 19th centuries. The decline in residential use in favour of business use must have occurred during the 18th century. The arrangement of shops on the ground floor still relates very closely to the 16th century pattern.

13 Restoration work in the 1850's (following the collapse of Lord Balmerino's house) and again in the 1880's rationalized the layout of the shop floor, removed the ruinous rear chamber of the backland on the second floor, strengthened the rear walls, added an additional attic room on the south elevation, installed the John Knox stained glass window, and repaired the panelling in the Oak Room, particularly on the north wall. In the 1853 restoration the coat of arms was discovered on the west facade and some of the existing 17th century tiles were probably transferred from other houses which were being demolished. The painted ceiling was recorded but not uncovered. Hippolyte Blanc's note of 1886 reviewing the work of 1853 is important –

'Though of slightly mixed character in detail, the wall panelling has every appearance of being genuine and fortunately is in perfect preservation.'

The panelling carries the date 1561 and is at least as important as the painted ceiling which may be early 17th century. The ceiling was uncovered in the 1970's.

14 In 1990/91 the 1556 walls and ceiling were uncovered in the foreland and left exposed. 16th century book pages were found pasted on the ground floor ceiling. The backland walls were also uncovered, surveyed and then covered up again. For the first time in its history the whole of John Knox House was accurately surveyed and recorded. Among the hitherto unknown features were a roll-moulded fireplace in the attic house similar to those in the main rooms (1556), blocked up windows on the south and east walls of the backland, continuous masonry construction linking the facade to the main structure of the foreland, and a 'squinch' supporting the turnpike stair on the south wall.

JOHN KNOX

1513	John Knox was born in the Giffordgate, Haddington. His father was a craftsman (owning his own business). His mother was related to a local landowning family. They were people of the 'middling kind'.
1520–36	Knox was educated at Haddington Grammar School and then at St Andrew's University where he was taught by John Major, one of Europe's leading intellectuals.
15 April 1536	Knox is ordained a priest at the early age of 22 but does not obtain a benefice. He becomes a notary public or lawyer.
1543/45	Accepted post of minor priest at Longniddry – augmented his income by tutoring children of wealthy families – became influenced by George Wishart, the Protestant Reformer.
1546	On 1 March George Wishart was burned at the stake in St Andrews. The Protestant Movement went underground. On 29 May Cardinal Beaton was murdered by Protestant rebels.
1547	Knox was training his pupils for entrance exams at St Andrews University when he was invited into St Andrews Castle becoming involved with the rebels. He was taken prisoner by the French and made a galley slave for 19 months.
1549	Released from galleys in France, he arrived in England. Appointed Chaplain to Berwick Parish Church. The Church of England at that time was dominated by Protestants. Then to Newcastle and Amersham, Buckinghamshire.
1553	Fled to the Continent with many other Protestants when Mary Tudor, who was an ardent Catholic, came to the throne of England. At this time he made his way to Geneva and came under the influence of Calvin and other leading Protestants.
1555/56	Returned to Scotland and married his first wife, Marjorie Bowes, fifth daughter of Richard Bowes of Aske, County Durham, (Captain of the Hold of Norham).

1556		In July he returned to Geneva as Minister at the Temple of Notre Dame La Neuve.
1557		In his absence, the Provincial Council in Edinburgh condemned him as a heretic and burned his effigy at the stake. His first son, Nathaniel, was born in May.
1558		Published *First Blast of the Trumpet against the Monstrous Regiment of Women.*
		In June he received the freedom of the City of Geneva. His second son, Eleazer, was born in November.
1559	January	left Geneva for Scotland.
	May	arrived in Scotland.
	July	elected minister at Edinburgh and preached in the Collegiate Church of St Giles, twice each Sunday and at least three times during the week.
	September	his wife, Marjorie Bowes, and his two sons arrived from Geneva.
1560	March	Mass was said for the last time in St Giles.
	August	Abolition by the Scottish Parliament of the jurisdiction of the Pope, in Scotland. Shared in production of The First Book of Discipline and The Scots Confession.
	December	Death of his wife, Marjorie Bowes.
1561	August	Mary, Queen of Scots, 18 years of age, landed at Leith. Knox's first interview with Queen Mary (at Holyrood).
1562	December	Knox attacks Mary's dancing in sermon. Second interview with Queen Mary.
1563	April	His third interview with Queen Mary (at Holyrood).
	June	His fourth interview with Queen Mary (at Holyrood).
	December	Tried for High Treason at Holyrood before the Privy Council, presided over by Queen Mary. Acquitted.
1564	Palm Sunday	Married Margaret Stewart, aged 17, daughter of Andrew, Lord Ochiltree. They had three daughters, Martha, Margaret and Elizabeth Knox.

1565	July	Marriage of Queen Mary, 22 years old, to cousin Henry Stuart, Lord Darnley.
1567	February	Lord Darnley murdered.
	July	Abdication of Queen Mary, aged 24, after imprisonment in Loch Leven Castle. Preached at Stirling at Coronation of James VI. The Earl of Moray appointed Regent.
	December	Preached at Opening of Parliament. Statutes of 1560 ratified and Reformed Church declared the only Church within the Realm of Scotland.
1570	February	Preached in St Giles, a Funeral Sermon for the Earl of Moray, Queen Mary's half-brother, 'The Good Regent' of Scotland. Knox's most powerful supporter, he had been assassinated at Linlithgow on 23 January.
	Autumn	John Knox struck by 'apoplexy'.
1572	November	John Knox preached in St Giles for the last time, at the induction of his successor, James Lawson, Vice-Principal of the University of Aberdeen. Death of John Knox, possibly in John Knox House. Funeral. His eulogy was pronounced by the Earl of Morton, now Regent of Scotland, at the open grave beside St Giles Church: 'There lies one who neither feared nor flattered any flesh.'

JAMES MOSSMAN

1	20 May 1492	John Mossman made a burgess for the making of the road or street of Nicholas Spethy at the Church of the Field. (= James' grandfather. James became a burgess on 3 October 1558 by right of his father John).
2	1525	First minute book of Goldsmiths' Craft, No. 4 Alan Mossman, No.12 Thomas Mossman, No. 19 John Mossman, No. 23 Alexander Mossman, No. 40 James Mossman, No. 47 James Cockie, No. 48 John Mossman, No. 57 John Mossman, No. 59 Thomas Mossman, No. 66 John Mossman, No. 67 James Mossman.
3	1529	John Mossman married to Marion Harlaw (previously married to Patrick Thomas).
4	24 August 1539	John Mossman appointed 'Wardone of our soverane lordis cunze for all the dais of his lyfe' (*Register of the Privy Seal of Scotland*).
5	1540	Duchess of Lorraine (aunt of Marie de Guise, wife to James V) sends miners to Scotland to work under the supervision of John Mossman to mine gold on Crawford Muir for the refashioning of the Scottish Crown and the making of a Crown Matrimonial by Mossman. John Roytell, French master mason, comes on the same ship.
6	1 March 1543	John Mossman reappointed Keeper of the Mint by Marie de Guise after death of James V.
7	Early 1550s	Death of Marion Harlaw. John Mossman marries Isobel Dee.
8	1556	James Mossman marries Mariota Arres. Major transfer of property includes Mariota's 'land' at The Netherbow.

9 1556–1557   At this time the house is reconstructed with a Renaissance facade which is perhaps the work of John Roytell, now the Royal Master Mason and another member like Mossman of the artistic circle patronized by Marie de Guise.

10 9 November 1557   Walter Mossman (son of John) appointed Warden of the Mint.

11 3 October 1558   James Mossman becomes a burgess, by right of his father John, who has died sometime in 1558.

12 5 October 1559   Walter Mossman and all the other officials of the Mint have resigned and are replaced due to the Protestant 'revolution'.

13 31 October 1561   Carved panel with lion rampant placed in house (Mary's return to Scotland 18 August 1561).

14 8 November 1561   James Mossman appointed Master Assayer of the Royal Mint.

15 1561–1566   Mossman undertakes several commissions for Mary Queen of Scots, and is knighted.

16 1567   Mary's forced abdication.

17 May 1568   Sir William Kirkcaldy of Grange holds Edinburgh Castle for Queen Mary.

18 26 July 1568   James and Mariota transfer the house to their son John, retaining the liferent to themselves.

19 30 September 1570 James and Mariota buy land in Currie.

20 Late 1570   Mariota dies.

21 23 February 1571   James about to marry Janet King, daughter of Alexander King the notary.
                      The house is transferred back from John to James and Janet King.

22 May 1571   John Knox leaves Edinburgh for St Andrews due to illness and the siege of Edinburgh Castle by the Earl of Morton.

23 24 April 1572   Thomas Acheson appointed 'Master Assayer of his graces and cunye and money in succession to James Mossman, who has not only ceased from the said

office but has conveyed himself within the Castle of Edinburgh and there remains with our sovereign lord's rebels and declared traitors, devising and forging false and counterfeit cunye within the same'. (*Register of the Privy Seal of Scotland*).

From this date Mossman is outlawed and made forfeit.

Janet King was also probably in the castle along with other wives.

24 29 June 1572	Gift to Captain Walter Aikman of the 'escheat' of the goods of James Mossman, goldsmith.
25 August 1572	John Knox returns to Edinburgh during a truce in the siege of the castle. (31 July to the end of the year. Knox dies on 24 November 1572).
26 14 March 1573	'Legitimation of James, Andrew and Agnes Aikman illegitimate children of the deceased Captain Walter Aikman and Marion Pott AND Gift to the same of the escheat of the goods of James Mossman, goldsmith burgess of Edinburgh, become in will, fugitive or at the horn for taking part with Sir William Kirkcaldy sometime of Grange, William Maitland the younger, sometime of Lethington, and other declared traitors in holding the Burgh and Castle of Edinburgh against the king, furnishing them with victuals and otherwise intercommuning with them, coming to the fields with displayed banners against the king's authority, slaughter and mutilation of faithful lieges.' (*Register of the Privy Seal of Scotland*).
27 2 May 1573	Gift to John Carmichael of Carmichael (kinsman of George Douglas of Parkhead) of property confiscated from James Mossman, including houses in Forrester's Wynd, Libberton Wynd, the Overbow and

	the Netherbow and land in Linlithgow and Currie. Carmichael is captain of one hundred light horse. (*Register of the Great Seal of Scotland*).
28 May 1573	Surrender of Edinburgh Castle.
29 3 August 1573	Kirkcaldy of Grange, James Cockie and James Mossman convicted of treason – 'harled in two carts backward from the Abbey to the cross' and hanged (*Diurnal of Occurrents*). According to the Register, 'hangit on the 3rd of August and their heads put up upon the castle wall'.
30	Gradually Janet King regained at least some of the property which had been held jointly in her name.
	Perhaps the house in the Netherbow was regained first though it is interesting that even in 1600 a Douglas (Lady Johnson) occupied the 'principal dwelling-house'. In 1581 the lands in Linlithgow were regained, in 1592 those in Currie.
31 1585–6	John Mossman (nephew of James and a Protestant supporter) makes the Roseneath communion cups.
32 May 1600	Janet King gives up her interest in the house which is transferred to a number of owners including her stepson John Mossman.